DICTION OF 4-Letter Words

WORDS YOU SHOULD KNOW

MANIK JOSHI

Dedication

THIS BOOK IS

DEDICATED

TO THOSE

WHO REALIZE

THE POWER OF ENGLISH

AND WANT TO

LEARN IT

SINCERELY

Copyright Notice

All rights reserved. Please note that the content in this book is protected under copyright law. This book is for your personal use only. No part of this book may be reproduced, stored in a retrieval system, or transmitted, in any form or by any means, electronic, mechanical, recording, or otherwise, without the prior written permission of the author.

Copyright Holder -- Manik Joshi
License -- Standard Copyright License
Year of Publication -- 2021
Email -- manik85joshi@gmail.com

****

IMPORTANT NOTE

This Book is Part of a Series
SERIES Name: "Words by Number of Letters"
[A Ten-Book Series]
BOOK Number: 01
BOOK Title: "Dictionary of 4-Letter Words"
****

Table of Contents

DICTIONARY OF 4-Letter Words 1
Dedication 2
Copyright Notice 3
4-Letter Words 5
4-Letter Words -- A 6
4-Letter Words -- B 10
4-Letter Words -- C 20
4-Letter Words -- D 25
4-Letter Words -- E 31
4-Letter Words -- F 33
4-Letter Words -- G 38
4-Letter Words -- H 43
4-Letter Words -- I 47
4-Letter Words -- J 49
4-Letter Words -- K 50
4-Letter Words -- L 51
4-Letter Words -- M 56
4-Letter Words -- N 60
4-Letter Words -- O 62
4-Letter Words -- P 64
4-Letter Words -- Q 70
4-Letter Words -- R 71
4-Letter Words -- S 77
4-Letter Words -- T 85
4-Letter Words -- U 89
4-Letter Words -- V 91
4-Letter Words -- W 93
4-Letter Words -- X, Y, Z 96
About the Author 97
BIBLIOGRAPHY 98

4-Letter Words

Letter A -- **41** 4-Letter Words
Letter B -- **50** 4-Letter Words
Letter C – **38** 4-Letter Words
Letter D -- **37** 4-Letter Words
Letter E -- **13** 4-Letter Words
Letter F -- **31** 4-Letter Words
Letter G -- **31** 4-Letter Words
Letter H -- **22** 4-Letter Words
Letter I -- **09** 4-Letter Words
Letter J -- **09** 4-Letter Words
Letter K -- **06** 4-Letter Words
Letter L -- **29** 4-Letter Words
Letter M -- **26** 4-Letter Words
Letter N -- **10** 4-Letter Words
Letter O -- **11** 4-Letter Words
Letter P -- **35** 4-Letter Words
Letter Q -- **03** 4-Letter Words
Letter R -- **28** 4-Letter Words
Letter S -- **50** 4-Letter Words
Letter T -- **23** 4-Letter Words
Letter U -- **05** 4-Letter Words
Letter V -- **09** 4-Letter Words
Letter W -- **26** 4-Letter Words
Letter XYZ -- **08** 4-Letter Words

TOTAL -- 550 Useful 4-Letter Words

SYMBOLS USED IN THIS DICTIONARY
adj. -- adjective // adv. -- adverb // n. -- noun // prep. -- preposition // pron. -- pronoun // v. -- verb // sb -- somebody // sth -- something

4-Letter Words -- A

01 -- abet [v.] -- to help or encourage or support sb to do sth wrong or illegal

02 -- able [adj.] -- skillful or good at sth [*synonyms*: talented, proficient]

03 -- ably [adv.] -- skillfully, successfully and well: [*synonym*: competently]

04 -- abut [v.] -- (of an area of land or a building) to be next to sth or to have a common boundary with the side of sth [*synonym*: adjoin]

05 -- ache [v.] -- *(a).* to feel continuous pain in a part of your body [*synonym*: hurt] | *(b).* to have a strong desire for sb/sth or to do sth | *(c).* to be very sad or distressed || **[n.]** a continuous feeling of pain in a part of your body

06 -- achy [adj.] -- affected by an uninterrupted pain that is small in degree

07 -- acid [n.] -- a liquid chemical, that has a sour taste, contains hydrogen and has a pH of less than seven | **[adj.]** -- *(a).* having a bitter sharp taste like that of a lemon [*synonym*: sour] | *(b).* (of sb's remarks) critical, rude and unkind [*synonym*: sarcastic]

08 -- acme [n.] -- the highest point or stage of development, achievement or the most excellent example of sth [*synonyms*: peak, summit, zenith]

09 -- acne [n.] -- a skin condition that is characterized by many pimples on the face and neck

10 -- acre [n.] -- a unit for measuring an area of land which is equal to 4840 square yards (4000 square meters)

11 -- aged [adj.] -- *(a).* [not before noun] of the specified age | *(b).* very old; grown old [*synonym*: matured] || **[n.]** *(the aged)* very old people

12 -- agog [adj.] -- [not before noun] showing extreme excitement, curiosity and interest to find out sth [*synonym*: eager]

13 -- ahoy [excl.] -- a word used by people in boats to attract attention from a distance

14 -- aide [n.] -- a person who helps or assists an important person, especially a politician or a leader, in their job [*synonym*: assistant]

15 -- airy [adj.] -- *(a).* with plenty of fresh air because of being spacious and open to the air [*synonyms*: breezy; well-ventilated] | *(b).* high in the air | *(c).* of air [*synonym*: atmospheric] | *(d).* showing no worry about sth or not treating sth as serious | *(e).* not serious or practical

16 -- ajar [adj.] -- [not before noun] (of a door or other opening) partly or slightly open: almost shut

17 -- akin [adj.] -- *(a).* having some of the essential same qualities [*synonym*: similar] | *(b).* related by blood

18 -- alas [exc.] -- used to show sadness, grief, regret or pity

19 -- alms [n.] -- sth such as money, food, clothes or other material given freely to poor people

20 -- also [adv.] -- (not used with negative verbs) in addition; as well; [*synonyms*: furthermore, too]

21 -- alum [n.] -- a chemical substance containing aluminum used to change the color of sth

22 -- amid (prep.) -- *(a).* in the middle or course of sth | *(b).* surrounded by sth.

23 -- amok [adv.] -- without self-control

24 -- anew [adv.] -- *(a).* again but in a new or different and more positive way | *(b).* once more [*synonym*: again]

25 -- anon [adv.] -- soon or shortly

26 -- ante [n.] -- a sum of money paid by a player in poker before receiving cards || **[v.]** -- to put a sum of money in poker before receiving cards

27 -- anti [prep.] -- opposed to; against || **[adj.]** -- opposed || **[n.]** -- a person who opposes a particular activity, idea, or policy, etc.

28 -- apex [n.] -- the top or highest part or point of sth: most important or successful part of sth [*synonyms*: peak, summit]

29 -- aqua [n.] -- *(a).* water | *(b).* a light bluish-green colour [*synonym*: aquamarine]

30 -- Arab [n.] -- *(a).* a person born or living in Arabia | *(b).* a horse of a breed from Arabia

31 -- arch [v.] -- *(a).* (of part of your body) to move and form a curved shape | *(b).* to be in a curved line or shape across or over sth || **[adj.]** -- [usually before noun] seeming amused because you are more aware of the situation than others || **[n.]** -- *(a).* anything that forms a curved shape at the top | *(b).* the raised part of the foot that is formed by a curved section of bones | *(c).* a curved structure on a bridge or the upper part of a building | *(d).* a structure with a curved top, especially at the entrance of the building

32 -- arid [adj.] -- *(a)*. (of land or a climate) very dry and having insufficient, little, or no rain to support agriculture or vegetation [*synonym*: parched] | *(b)*. with nothing new, exciting or interesting in it

33 -- arms [n.] -- weapons, especially as used by the defense forces [*synonym*: weaponry]

34 -- atom [n.] -- the smallest part of a chemical element that can exist [*synonym*: particle]

35 -- atop [prep.] -- on the top of || **[adv.] --** on the top

36 -- aura [n.] -- the distinct and noticeable quality or feeling that seems to surround a person or place or come from sb or sth

37 -- aver [v.] -- to state firmly that sth is certainly true [*synonyms*: assert, avow]

38 -- avid [adj.] -- [usually before noun] having or showing extreme interest, eagerness or enthusiasm about sth, often a hobby [*synonym*: keen]

39 -- avow [v.] -- to publicly express your opinion about sth in a firm way [*synonym*: affirm]

40 -- awed [adj.] -- filled with a strong feeling of great respect, surprise and slight fear [*synonym*: overwhelmed]

41 -- awry [adj.] -- away from the usual or intended course [*synonym*: amiss] | out of the normal position [*synonym*: askew] || **[adv.] --** in a position that is not normal and turned toward one side

4-Letter Words -- B

01 -- babe [n.] -- *(a).* *(slang)* a word used to address a young woman, your wife or lover to show affection | *(b).* an attractive young woman

02 -- baby [n.] -- *(a).* an extremely young child or animal; an infant | *(b).* the youngest member of a family or group | *(c).* a person who behaves like an extremely young child and easily gets upset | *(d).* *(slang)* a word used to address a young woman, your wife or lover to show affection || **[adj.] --** (of vegetables) small-sized version of a particular vegetable; that are picked when they are very small | **[v.] --** to treat sb as if they were a baby; to give too much care to sb

03 -- back [n.] -- *(a).* the rear part of the body that is opposite to the chest, between the neck to bottom | *(b).* the row of bones that are located in the middle of the back | *(c).* the last few pages of a book, magazine, newspaper, etc. | *(d).* the area, side or part of sth that is to the farthest away from the front | *(e).* the part of sth against which you lean your head or other body parts for support | *(f).* (in sports) a player who has been assigned the task of defending their team's goal | *(g).* the part of sth (such as a sheet) that is on the opposite side to the one that is in front || **[adj.] --** *(a).* of or from a period of past time | *(b).* located behind or on the opposite side to sth | *(c).* owed for a time in the past | *(d).* (of a vowel) that is pronounced with the back of the tongue in a higher position than the front || **[adv.] --** *(a).* behind you; opposite | *(b).* prevented from coming out | *(c).* at a distance or direction farther away | *(d).* at a place or state that is previously left or asserted | *(e)*. to or into the place, condition, situation or activity where sb/sth was before | *(f)*. in return, reply or response | *(g)*. in or into the past; before or ago || **[v.]** -- *(a)*. to move or make sth move further away | *(b)*. to be located behind sth | *(c)*. to cover the back of sth to support or protect it | *(d)*. to help, assist or support to sb/sth | *(e)*. to play or sing music to support the main singer or instrument | *(f)*. to bet money on sth such as a horse in a race, a team in a contest, etc.

04 -- **bait [n.]** -- *(a)*. food items, fixed to a hook to catch fish or placed in nets, traps, etc. to attract and catch birds or animals | *(b)*. a person or thing that is used to catch or trap sb or to attract them so that they can act according to your wishes [*synonym*: inducement] || **[v.]** -- *(a)*. to place food items on a hook to catch fish or in nets, traps, etc. to attract and catch birds or animals [*synonym*: entice] | *(b)*. to make cruel or insulting remarks intentionally in order to make sb angry

05 -- **bake [v.]** -- *(a)*. to cook food in an oven or on heated metal in dry heat; to be cooked in this way | *(b)*. to become or to make sth (such as bricks, earthenware, etc.) become hard by heating | *(c)*. to be or become extremely hot

06 -- **bald [adj.]** -- *(a)*. having little or no hair on the scalp of the head [*synonym*: hairless] | *(b)*. without any of the natural or usual growth of hair, marks, vegetation, etc. on the skin or surface of sth | *(c)*. not having extra explanation or detail to help you understand what is being mentioned [*synonyms*: blunt, plain]

07 -- bale [n.] -- a large amount of light material such as paper, hay, or cotton pressed tightly together and tied up using cords, wires, etc. for shipping, storage, or sale || **[v.]** -- to make sth into bales

08 -- ball [n.] -- *(a).* a solid or hollow round, a spherical or egg-shaped object used for throwing, hitting or kicking in games and sports | *(b).* a round object or a thing that has been formed into a round shape | *(c).* a hit, kick or throw of the solid or hollow round, spherical or egg-shaped object in games and sports | *(d).* a large formal party that involves dancing || **[v.]** -- to form sth (by squeezing, etc.) or be formed into a rounded shape

09 -- balm [n.] -- *(a).* an aromatic cream used to soothe the wound [*synonym*: ointment] | *(b).* sth that has a comforting or soothing effect [*synonym*: solace]

10 -- band [n.] -- *(a).* a range of radio waves | *(b).* a small group of musicians playing music, often with singers | *(c).* a group of musicians playing brass and percussion instruments | *(d).* a thin flat strip or circle put around sth in order to hold them together or to strengthen them | *(e).* a strip of color or material on sth that is not like from what is around it | *(f).* a group of people with same opinions or who do sth together | *(g).* a range of numbers, ages, prices, etc. to count or measure people or things || **[v.]** -- *(a).* [usually passive] to put a strip of a different color or material around sth | *(b).* to be organized into a range of price, income, etc. to count or measure people or things

11 -- bane [n.] -- sth that causes trouble, distress, worry or annoyance and makes sb unhappy

12 -- bang [v.] -- (a). to hit or strike sth in a way that makes a sudden, short, loud noise | **(b).** to close sth or to be closed with a sudden, short, loud noise | **(c).** to hit hard and noisily sth, especially a part of the body, against sth by accident [*synonyms*: bump; knock] | **(d).** to handle, or put, push, throw sth somewhere with a lot of force and in a sudden manner [*synonym*: slam] | **(e).** *(slang)* (of a man) to make a physical relationship with a woman || **[n.] -- (a).** a sudden, short loud noise | **(b).** a sudden, short, strong painful blow, knock or hit, especially on a part of the body || **[adv.] --** directly; exactly; completely || **(excl.) --** used to sound like the noise of a gun, etc.

13 -- bank [n.] -- (a). an organization engaged in financial services where people keep their money or lend money from | **(b).** a supply of money or things that are used as money in the game of gambles | **(c).** a mass of sth such as cloud or snow formed by the wind | **(d).** a row or series of similar machines, etc. | **(e).** the side of a water body such as a lake, river, canal, etc. and the land near it | **(f).** a raised area of ground sloping at the sides | **(g).** storage of sth that is ready for use | **(h).** an artificial slope built at the side of a road || **[v.] -- (a).** to put money into a bank account | **(b).** to have an account with a particular bank or similar organization that is engaged in financial services | **(c).** to pass through with one side higher than the other when you are turning | **(d).** to put a large amount of burning material such as coal on fire so that the fire burns in a slow manner for a long time | **(e).** to form sth into heaps or piles

14 -- barb [n.] -- *(a).* the point of an arrow, a hook or a similar subject curved backward and is difficult to be pulled out | *(b).* a remark that intended to hurt sb's feelings

15 -- bard [n.] -- sb who writes poems [*synonym*: poet]

16 -- bare [adj.] -- *(a).* not covered by any clothes | *(b).* (of surfaces) not covered with anything; not protected or secured with anything | *(c).* (of a room, cupboard, etc.) with no things inside | *(d).* (of trees or countryside) not having leaves; not having plants or trees | *(e).* [only before noun] just enough; of the most basic or simple type || **[v.]** -- to remove the covering from sth; to remove clothes from part of the body

17 -- barf [v.] -- to vomit || **[n.]** -- food or other substance that has been vomited

18 -- bark [n.] -- *(a).* the outer covering of a tree or plant | *(b).* the short loud sound produced by some animals, especially dogs | *(c).* a short loud sound produced by a gun || **[v.]** -- *(a).* (of dogs) to make a short loud sound | *(b).* to give orders, ask sth, etc. in a loud and unfriendly manner | *(c).* to rub the skin off your body part, such as the knee, etc. by knocking against sth or by falling

19 -- barn [n.] -- *(a).* a large farm building used to store grain or keep animals | *(b).* a large building that looks plain ugly | *(c).* a shelter to keep unused buses, trucks, etc

20 -- bash [n.] -- *(a).* a hard and strong hit | *(b).* a large party or celebration || **[v.]** -- *(a).* to hit sb/sth very hard | *(b).* to strongly criticize sb/sth

21 -- **bask** **[v.]** -- to lie or sit and enjoy heat or light of sth, especially the sun

22 -- **bawl** **[v.]** -- *(a).* to shout unpleasantly, angrily or loudly | *(b).* to cry unpleasantly, unpleasantly or loudly

23 -- **beak** **[n.]** -- *(a).* the hard curved or pointed part of a bird's mouth [*synonym*: bill] | *(b).* a person's large and/or pointed nose | *(c). (slang)* -- a person, especially a judge, who is in a position of authority

24 -- **beam** **[v.]** -- *(a).* [no passive] to have a big happy smile on your face because of pleasure, pride, etc. | *(b).* to send out radio or television signals using electronic equipment | *(c).* to send out a stream of light or/and produce heat || **[n.]** -- *(a).* a line or stream of light, electric waves or particles | *(b).* a long piece of wood, metal, stone, etc. used to support the weight of a roof, building, etc. | *(c).* a big and happy smile

25 -- **bean** **[n.]** -- *(a).* an edible seed, or pod containing edible seeds, of a climbing plant | *(b).* (in compounds) seed from some plants, especially coffee plants || **[v.]** -- to hit or strike sb on the head

26 -- **bear** **[n.]** -- *(a).* a type of heavily built wild animal with thick fur and sharp claws | *(b).* a trader selling shares in a company, etc, with the hope to buy them back later at a lower price || **bear** **[v.]** -- *(a).* (used with the modal verb can/could in negative and interrogative sentences) to be able to accept and handle sth unpleasant | *(b).* to not be appropriate of fitting for sth | *(c).* to go, move or turn in the direction that is mentioned | *(d).* to support the weight of sb/sth | *(e).* to have a negative feeling | *(f).* to be responsible for sth | *(g).* to produce a child | *(h).* to produce fruit or flowers |

(i). to carry sth with an intention to show it to other people | *(j).* to carry sb/sth while making a movement | *(k).* to act, behave or move in a particular manner | *(l).* to have a particular name

27 -- beat [v.] -- *(a).* to defeat sb in a game, competition, war, sports game, etc. | *(b).* to be in command of sth [*synonym*: defeat] | *(c).* to make, or cause sth to make, a regular pattern of sounds or movements | *(d).* to change the shape of metal by repeatedly hitting it with a tool such as a hammer | *(e).* to keep away from sth *(f).* to be too difficult for sb to understand, solve, etc. [*synonym*: defeat] | *(g).* to be more effective than sth else | *(h).* to repeatedly and violently strike or hit sb/sth very hard using hand, whip, club, etc. [*synonym*: pound] | *(i).* to mix sth (such as eggs, cream, etc.) thoroughly in short quick movements using a fork, etc. | *(j).* to make a path by walking somewhere or over sth || **[n.] --** *(a).* a single blow or series of regular blows to drum and sound thereof; the rhythmic movement(s) of a bird's wings, heart, etc. and the sound thereof | *(b).* the area in which a police or security personnel walks around on a regular basis because he/she is responsible for keeping watch on unlawful activities there | *(c).* or a unit of rhythm, in a bar of a piece of music, or a poem, etc. || **[adj.] --** completely tired [*synonym*: exhausted]

28 -- beau [n.] -- a male lover or friend of a woman

29 -- beck [n.] -- a small river [*synonym*: stream]

30 -- beef [n.] -- *(a).* the flesh of a cow used as meat | *(b).* a complaint || **[v.] --** to complain a lot about sb/sth

31 -- bell [n.] -- *(a).* a device which makes a ringing sound | *(b).* sth that attracts your attention

32 -- bilk [v.] -- to cheat sb, especially by taking money from them in an unfair or dishonest manner [*synonyms*: con, swindle]

33 -- bird [n.] -- *(a).* two-legged, two-winged, feather-covered creature | *(b).* a person who seems to be strange or unusual in some way | *(c). (slang) --* an offensive way of referring to a girl or woman

34 -- blab [v.] -- to talk too much and tell sb sth that should be kept secret or hidden

35 -- blob [n.] -- *(a).* a small amount or drop of a thick liquid or sticky substance | *(b).* a small area of color

36 -- blot [v.] -- *(a).* to remove liquid from a surface by pressing paper, cloth or other soft material on it | *(a).* to make a spot or mark on sth. such as ink on paper or paint on clothing || **[n.] --** *(a).* a spot or mark on sth, such as made by ink, paint or dirt [*synonyms*: stain, splotch] | *(b).* a thing that spoils your reputation or happiness

37 -- blow [v.] -- *(a).* (of wind or air) to move | *(b).* to be moved by the wind, sb's breath, etc. | to move sth through wind or breath | *(c).* to break sth open with explosive substances | *(d).* to make or shape sth by sending out air | *(e).* to produce a sound by sending out air from the mouth into the whistle, musical instrument, etc. | *(f).* to reveal a secret | *(g).* to send out air from the mouth | *(h).* to spend or waste a lot of money on sth | *(i).* to waste an opportunity | *(j).* used to show your annoyance or surprise over sth or that you do not care about sth | *(k).* (of the fuse) to melt because of the strong electric current, causing electricity flow to stop | *(l).* (with respect to nose) to clear your nose by sending out air strongly through it | *(m).* (with respect to kiss) to kiss your hand and then act as if to send out the kiss towards sb through air | *(n). (slang)* to leave a place suddenly || **[n.]** -- *(a).* a hard hit with the hand, a weapon, etc. | *(b).* sadness- or disappointment-causing sudden and unpleasant event | *(c).* the action of forcefully sending out air from your mouth

38 -- blub [v.] -- to cry in a noisy and uncontrollable way [*synonym*: sob]

39 -- bong [n.] -- a low-pitched, deep, clear sound that continues for a long time and is made by a large bell || **[v.] --** (of a large bell) to produce a sound that is low-pitched, deep, clear and continues for a long time

40 -- boob [n.] -- *(a).* a stupid mistake | *(b).* a person that lacks intelligence | *(c). (slang) --* a woman's breast || **[v.] --** to make a stupid mistake

41 -- boon [n.] -- sth that is very helpful and makes life easier for you [*synonym*: windfall]

42 -- boor [n.] -- a rude, rough, bad-mannered and unpleasant person [*synonym*: lout]

43 -- boss [n.] -- *(a).* a person whose job is to give orders to others or tell them what to do at work [*synonyms*: employer, supervisor, manager] | *(b).* a person who is in charge of a large organization || **[adj.]** *(slang) --* very good || **[v.] --** to tell sb what to do in an aggressive and/or annoying way

44 -- bout [n.] -- *(a).* a short period of intense or great activity of a particular kind, usually sth unpleasant such as binging, fighting, etc. | *(b).* a short period of time during which someone suffers from illness or disease, etc.

45 -- brag [v.] -- to talk very proudly about sth that you own or have done or have an ability to do [*synonyms*: boast, swank] || **[n.]** -- *(a).* a gambling card game which is a simple form of poker | *(b).* sth that sb talks about proudly, often to appear more important, intelligent, or clever, etc. than others

46 -- brat [n.] -- a child, who behaves in an ill-manner and can't be managed easily [*synonym*: monster]

47 -- brim [v.] -- to be full of sth; to fill sth || **[n.]** -- *(a).* the top or upper edge of a cup, bowl, glass, or other container | *(b).* the flat, projecting edge around the bottom of a hat

48 -- buff [n.] -- *(a).* a person takes a lot of interest in a particular subject or activity and knows a lot about it | *(b).* a pale yellow-brown color [*synonym*: beige] | *(c).* a soft, thick, strong yellowish-brown leather || **[adj.]** -- *(a).* pale yellow-brown in color [*synonym*: beige] | *(b).* (slang) -- physically fit, attractive and good-looking with big/huge muscles || **[v.]** -- to polish sth with a soft cloth

49 -- burp [n.] -- a noisy release of gas through the mouth || **[v.]** -- *(a).* to noisily release air from the stomach through the mouth | *(b).* to cause (a baby) to bring up air from the stomach by rubbing or patting its back after feeding

50 -- busk [v.] -- to perform music or other entertainment in the street or another public place and ask for money from people passing by

4-Letter Words -- C

01 -- cage [n] -- a box-type structure of metal bars or wire to keep animals or birds, often for displaying to the public || **[v.]** -- [usually passive] to keep or put an animal or bird in a cage [*synonyms*: enclose, confine]

02 -- calf [n.] -- *(a).* the fleshy back part of the human leg between the ankle and the knee | *(b).* a young cow or bull; the young of an elephant, whale or other large animals

03 -- cant [n.] -- insincere statements or talks especially about moral, political or religious nature [*synonym*: hypocrisy] || **[v.]** -- *(a).* to be or put sth in a sloping position [*synonym*: tilt] | *(b).* to talk insincerely about moral, political or religious matters

04 -- carp [n.] -- a large freshwater fish used for food || **[v.]** -- to keep complaining or criticizing about sb/sth in an annoying or quarrelsome way [*synonyms*: grumble, grouse]

05 -- cede [v.] -- to unwillingly give up your right, power, territory, etc. to sb [*synonyms*: concede, yield]

06 -- cert [n.] -- a thing that is definite to occur or be successful [*synonym*: certainty]

07 -- chap [n.] -- a man or boy who is your friend or fellow [*synonym*: guy]

08 -- char [n.] -- *(a).* material that has been burned partially | *(b).* a woman employed as a cleaner in a house, office or building, etc. || **[v.]** -- *(a).* to become black by burning slightly or partially; to make sth black by burning it slightly or partially [*synonyms*: scorch, singe] | *(b).* to work as a cleaner in a house

09 -- chef [n.] -- a professional cook

10 -- chic [adj.] -- very fashionable or stylish [*synonym*: elegant] || **[n.] --** a perfectly dressed, fashionable or stylish woman

11 -- chit [n.] -- *(a).* officially written and signed short note or slip of paper, giving sb permission to do sth, or showing an amount of money that is owed [*synonyms*: receipt, voucher] | *(b).* a young woman or girl, without any regard for older people

12 -- chop [v.] -- *(a).* to cut sth into pieces with a knife, axe or other sharp tools | *(b).* to hit sb/sth with a quick, heavy, short downward blow or stroke | *(c).* [usually passive] to reduce sth by a large amount || **[n.] --** *(a).* a thick slice of meat with a piece of bone in it | *(b).* an act of cutting sth with a quick, heavy downward blow or stroke with a knife, axe or other sharp tools

13 -- chow [n.] -- *(a).* food | *(b).* a dog of a Chinese breed with long thick hair, a broad muzzle, a curled tail and a bluish-black tongue

14 -- chug [v.] -- *(a).* (of a machine or engine) to make short repeated sounds while it is working, moving or running slowly | *(b).* (slang) -- to drink all of the sth quickly without stopping || **[n.] --** short repeated sounds made by working, moving or running machine or engine

15 -- chum [n.] -- a close friend

16 -- clad [adj.] -- *(a).* (of people) wearing a particular type of dress or clothing [*synonym*: dressed] | *(b).* (of things) covered with a particular type of thing, material, layer, etc.

17 -- **clam** *[v.]* -- to refuse to speak when sb asks you about sth || *[n].* a type of shellfish that can be eaten

18 -- **clan** *[n.]* -- a group of families who are closely related to each other: | *(b).* a very large family | *(c).* a group of people who are closely related because of particular interests, things, etc.

19 -- **clod** *[n.]* -- *(a).* a lump or mass of earth, clay or soil | *(b).* a stupid person

20 -- **clog** *[v.]* -- [often passive] to block or obstruct sth or to become blocked or obstructed making a movement or an activity difficult [*synonym*: choke] | *[n.]* -- any object that acts as a barrier or obstruction

21 -- **clot** *[v.]* -- (of blood or cream) to form thick or solid lumps as it dries; to cause blood to form into thick or solid lumps [*synonyms*: coagulate, congeal] || *[n.]* -- a lump formed by thick blood as it dries

22 -- **coax** *[v.]* -- to convince sb to do sth by talking to them kindly, gentle and patiently [*synonyms*: cajole, persuade]

23 -- **cock** *[n.]* -- *(a).* an adult male chicken, often bigger than hens; rooster | *(b).* a male of any other bird | *(c). (slang)* used as a friendly form of address between two people || *[v.]* -- to move, turn or raise a part of your body so that it is in a particular angle

24 -- **coir** *[n.]* -- a rough fibrous material made from the outer husk of the coconut, used for making ropes

25 -- **cope** *[v.]* -- to deal successfully with the difficult or problematic matter, situation or job [*synonyms*: handle, manage]

26 -- cord [n.] -- string or rope, often flexible or made from several twisted strands

27 -- coup [n.] -- *(a).* a change of government that occurs in a sudden, illegal and often violent way [*synonym*: rebellion] | *(b).* the fact or instance of achieving notable success in a way that seems to be very difficult [*synonym*: accomplishment]

28 -- cozy [adj.] *(a).* (especially of a space or an area) giving a feeling of warmth, comfort, protection or relaxation, because of being small and surrounded by walls or sides [*synonym*: snug] | *(b).* friendly, pleasant, and private | *(c).* easy, suitable, or fitting, but not always sincere or right || **[v.]** -- to make (sb) feel comfortable or unworried

29 -- crag [n.] -- a high, steep, rough rocky cliff or projecting part of a mountain

30 -- cram [v.] -- *(a).* to push or force sb/sth into a small space; to forcefully fill sth beyond its capacity | *(b).* to fill a small space or area, with a lot of people | *(c).* to learn a lot of things in a short time to prepare for an exam

31 -- crew [n.] -- *(a).* a group of people who work together on and operate a ship, aircraft, etc. | *(b).* a group of people with special skills who work closely together | *(c).* all the people working on a ship, plane, etc. apart from the officers who are in charge | *(d).* a group of people who row boats using oars in a race | *(e).* the sport of rowing using oars with other people in a racing boat | [*synonym*: squad] | *(f).* a group of people || **[v.]** -- to be part of a crew, especially on a ship or an aircraft; to provide an aircraft or a ship with a group of people to operate it.

32 -- **crow [n.]** -- *(a).* a black-colored, heavy-billed large bird, with a rough unpleasant cry | *(b).* shrill sounds like that of a cock or rooster || **[v.]** -- *(a).* (of a cock or rooster) to make repeated loud, shrill, high sounds, especially early in the morning | *(b).* (of a baby or infant) to make sounds that appear to be of pleasure | *(c).* to talk about your specific achievement in a very proud way, especially when sb else has failed [*synonyms*: boast, gloat]

33 -- **crud [n.]** -- any dirty or unpleasant substance

34 -- **crux [n.]** -- the decisive, most important, essential, serious or difficult part of a problem or an issue [*synonyms*: nub, essence]

35 -- **cull [v]** -- *(a).* to deliberately kill a number of animals in a group to control their population | *(b).* to gather parts, pieces, ideas, etc., from different places to use it for another purpose [*synonym*: pick]

36 -- **curb [v.]** -- to control or limit sth bad; to keep sth bad in check || **[n.]** -- sth that controls sth bad; sth that keeps sth in check bad [*synonym*: restraint]

37 -- **curt [adj.]** -- (of sb's manner, speech or behavior) impolite because involving very few words, or because done in a very quick way [*synonyms*: abrupt, brusque]

38 -- **cyst [n.]** -- a growth of membranous tissue containing air, fluid or other substance that forms in or on a person's or an animal's body [*synonyms*: carbuncle, swelling]

4-Letter Words -- D

01 -- **daft** [adj.] -- silly or senseless, often in an amusing way [*synonym*: insane]

02 -- **damp** [adj.] -- slightly wet in an unpleasant way [*synonym*: soggy] || [n.] -- the state of being slightly wet in an unpleasant way; areas in the structure of a building, etc. are slightly wet in an unpleasant way || [v.] -- *(a).* to make (sth) slightly wet in an unpleasant way | *(b).* to reduce the intensity of fire by reducing the flow of air to it

03 -- **dank** [adj.] -- (of cellars, caves, etc.) wet, cold and unpleasant [*synonym*: damp]

04 -- **darn** [v.] -- to repair or mend a hole in sth knitted or made of cloth, by sewing rows of stitches across the hole || [n.] -- a place on sth knitted or made of cloth that has been repaired by sewing rows of stitches

05 -- **dash** [n.] -- *(a).* an act of suddenly and/or quickly going somewhere | *(b).* an act of doing sth in a speedy way because of lack of time | *(c).* a type of race in which the participants run, swim, etc. hastily or very fast over a short distance [*synonym*: sprint] | *(d).* a small amount of sth that is added to sth else | *(e).* the mark (—) used to separate parts of a sentence | *(f).* dashboard of a car | *(g).* stylish, enthusiastic and confident behavior || [v.] -- *(a).* to go somewhere very quickly or/and suddenly [*synonym*: rush] | *(b).* to throw or strike sth violently onto sth, especially that has a hard surface; to make sth fall, hit or strike violently onto sth, especially that has hard surface [*synonym*: beat]

06 -- daub [v.] -- to spread a thick or sticky substance such as paint, mud, etc. onto sth in a careless way [*synonyms*: smear, splatter] || **[n.] --** *(a).* a mixture of clay, plaster, etc. used in for making walls, especially in the past | *(b).* a small amount of thick or sticky substance such as paint, mud, etc. that has been spread in a careless way | *(c).* a picture that has been painted badly

07 -- dead [adj.] -- *(a).* no longer alive or living; those who have died | *(b).* never having been alive | *(c).* lifeless [*synonym*: inanimate] | *(d).* belonging to the ancient times or earlier period; no longer practiced or fashionable | *(e).* no longer in use; being out of use; finished | *(f).* no longer active [*synonyms*: extinct, vanished] | *(g).* not capable of making any effect | *(h).* not able to be aware of feelings or emotions [*synonyms*: insensate, insensitive] | *(i).* extremely tired or lacking warmth; not well | *(j).* entire, absolute, complete or exact | *(k).* unproductive; infertile | *(l).* not running, flowing or circulating | *(m).* (of a belief or plan) no longer believed in or aimed/intended for | *(n).* (of a machine or equipment) not functioning because of a deficiency of power | *(o).* (of place) without activity or interest; very quiet [*synonym*: hushed] | *(p).* (of a part of the body) unable to feel or respond because of cold, etc. [*synonym*: numb] | *(q).* (of sb's face or voice) expressing no feeling or emotion [*synonyms*: expressionless, impassive, unresponsive] | *(r).* (in sport) not inside the playing area; out of the play | *(s).* (of business) without any activity of buying or selling || **(adv.] --** entirely; accurately or exactly; precisely

08 -- deaf [n.] -- (a). not able to hear, either completely or partly | **(b).** (the deaf) people who are unable to hear | **(c).** [not before noun] unwilling or refusing to listen or pay attention to sth

09 -- deed [n.] -- (a). a very good or bad thing that is done or performed by sb [*synonym*: act] | **(b).** a legal document signed by sb that officially proves their ownership of a property such as land, house or a building

10 -- deem [v.] -- (not usually used in the progressive tenses) to form or have a particular opinion about sth [*synonyms*: consider, judge]

11 -- deft [adj.] -- (a). (of a person's movements) effective, clever, skillful and quick [*synonyms*: adroit, nifty] | **(b).** skillful

12 -- defy [v.] -- (a). to unusually or unexpectedly and openly refuse to obey or show respect for a law, a rule, authority, etc. [*synonyms*: disregard, flout] | **(b).** (of a description, belief, understanding, etc.) to be impossible or almost impossible to believe, describe, or explain, etc. | **(c).** to resist or oppose sb/sth to a very unusual degree and in a successful manner [*synonym*: confront]

13 -- dent [v.] -- (a). to make a dip or hollow mark in a flat hard surface of sth, usually by hitting or pressurizing it but not breaking it [*synonym*: cavity | **(b).** to have a bad or damageable effect on sb's confidence, pride reputation, etc. || **[n.] -- (a).** a hollow dip or hollow mark in a flat hard surface of sth, usually by hitting or pressurizing it but not breaking it | **(b).** a bad or damageable effect on sb's confidence, pride reputation, etc.

14 -- deny [v.] -- (a). to say that sth is false [*synonym*: refute] | **(b).** to refuse to accept or admit sth [*synonym*: rebuff] | **(c).** to refuse to allow sb to have sth [*synonym*: disallow] | *(d).* to refuse to let yourself have sth for moral or religious reasons

15 -- dewy [adj.] -- wet with dew

16 -- diet [n.] -- *(a).* the food that you regularly or usually eat and drink | *(b).* certain foods especially in a limited variety or amount that you eat for medical reasons or in order to lose your weight; a time when you eat certain foods in a limited variety or amount | *(c).* a large amount of a restricted range of activities || **[v.] --** to eat less food or only certain kinds of food in order to lose weight

17 -- dime [n.] -- a ten-cent coin of the US and Canada

18 -- dine [v.] -- to eat dinner

19 -- dire [adj.] -- extremely serious, terrible, urgent, etc. [*synonym*: calamitous]

20 -- doff [v.] -- to take off or raise your hat to show respect for sb/sth

21 -- dole [n.] -- money or benefits that government pays to unemployed people

22 -- dolt [n.] -- a silly or foolish person

23 -- doom [n.] -- any unavoidable terrible event, fate or situation; death or destruction [*synonym*: destiny] || **[v.] --** [usually passive] to make sb/sth sure to suffer, die, or be unsuccessful, etc.

24 -- dork [n.] -- a boring, unstylish, awkward or silly person that is worth laughing at

25 -- doss -- [v.] *(a).* to sleep in rough accommodation or without a real bed | *(b).* to spend your time without any particular reason, purpose or effort | **[n.] --** *(a).* an instance of sleeping in rough accommodation or without a real bed | *(b).* sth that does not need much effort

26 -- doze [v.] -- to sleep lightly for a short time, usually during the day [*synonym*: slumber] || **[n.] --** a short period of sleep, usually during the day [*synonym*: slumber]

27 -- drab [adj.] -- *(a).* without brightness, spirit or interest; dull and boring in appearance [*synonym*: dowdy] | *(b).* of a dull light brown color

28 -- dual [adj.] -- [only before noun] having two parts or aspects

29 -- duct [n.] -- *(a).* a pipe or tube that carries liquid, gas, wires, etc. | *(b).* a tube in the body or in plants that carries fluid from one part to another [*synonyms*: channel, vessel]

30 -- duel [n.] -- *(a).* a formal fight or contest with weapons such as swords, guns, etc. between two people, to settle a disagreement or quarrel, especially over a matter of honor | *(b).* a competition, contest or struggle between two people or groups || **[v.] --** to fight or contest with weapons such as swords, guns, etc. to settle a disagreement or quarrel, especially over a matter of honor

31 -- duly [adv.] -- *(a).* in the correct, appropriate or expected manner | *(b).* at the expected, appropriate, arranged or correct time

32 -- dump [v.] -- *(a).* to throw away sth you do not want in an unsuitable place | *(b).* to leave sb/sth for sb else to take care of | *(c).* to dispose of goods by selling them at a very low price | *(d).* to put sth down in a quick, careless or untidy way | *(e).* to end a relationship that is related to love or romance | *(f).* (of computing) to copy information and store it somewhere || [n.] -- *(a).* a place to keep waste, trash, rubbish or garbage | *(b).* a temporary store for military supplies, especially weapons | *(c).* (of computing) an act of copying data; a copy of stored data | *(d).* a hill of waste sand formed due to piling of it during the production of gold || *(e).* a place that is very unpleasant or dirty

33 -- **dune** [n.] -- small hill or mound of sand or other sediment formed by the wind, near a sea beach or in a desert

34 -- **dung** [n.] -- solid waste or excrement from animals, especially cattle, horses, etc. [*synonyms*: compost, manure] || [v.] -- to drop or spread solid waste or excrement on a piece of ground

35 -- **dunk** [v.] -- *(a).* to put food (such as a cookie, bread, doughnut, etc.) quickly into coffee, milk, tea or other liquid before eating it [*synonym*: dip] | *(b).* to push sb jokingly underwater for a short time; to put sth into water [*synonym*: immerse] | *(c).* (in basketball) to jump very high and put the ball through the basket forcefully with the hands above the rim

36 -- **dupe** [v.] -- to cheat sb by tricking them into believing or doing sth [*synonyms*: con, deceive] || [n.] -- a person who is tricked or cheated

37 -- **dusk** [n.] -- the time of day when the sun has almost set and it is nearly dark [*synonym*: twilight]

4-Letter Words -- E

01 -- **each** [adv.] -- by, for or to every one of a group of two or more people or things (used after a noun or an amount) | [det.] -- used to refer to everyone in a group of two or more people or things, considered and identified separately | [pron.] -- everyone in a group of two or more people or things, considered and identified separately

02 -- **easy** [adj.] -- *(a).* achieved, done or obtained without great effort, difficulties or problems; not hard or difficult | *(b).* (of a period of time or way of life) free from care, discomfort, worry, pain, or trouble [*synonyms*: calm, comfortable, relaxed] | *(c).* [only before noun] unable to defend yourself from attack | *(d).* [only before noun] pleasant, friendly and welcoming | *(e).* (of women) willing to make physical relations with many different men || [adv.] -- used to tell sb to be alert or careful when doing sth

03 -- **eats** [n.] -- food, especially at a party

04 -- **ecru** [n.] -- a light brown or cream color

05 -- **eddy** [v.] -- (of air, dust, smoke, water, etc.) to move round and round in a circle [*synonym*: swirl] | [n.] -- a movement of air, dust, smoke, water, etc. in a circle [*synonyms*: vortex, whirlpool]

06 -- **edgy** [adj.] -- *(a).* nervous, worried, tense, upset and showing irritation [*synonym*: jittery] | *(b).* with sharp or pointed corners | *(c).* (of a book, movie, piece of music, or other artistic things) with a sharp exciting quality

07 -- **emit** [v.] -- to send out or let out sth such as light, heat, smell, sound, particles, gas, etc. [*synonyms*: discharge, release]

08 -- envy [v.] -- to be sad and restless over the good qualities, achievements, possessions, opportunities, fortune, etc. of sb and desire the same for you || **[n.] --** the feeling of wanting the same qualities, achievements, possessions, opportunities and fortune that sb else has [*synonym*: jealousy]

09 -- epic [adj.] -- *(a).* having the features of an epic (a long poem about the deeds of a great historical or well-known personality or about a history of a particular place, state or nation) | ***(b).*** occurring over a long period of time and with a lot of difficulties | ***(c).*** very great, inspiring and impressive || **[n.] -- *(a).*** a long poem about the great deeds of a historical or well-known personality or about a history of a particular place, state or nation; this style of poetry | ***(b).*** a long, difficult and praiseworthy job or activity

10 -- ergo (adv.] -- therefore

11 -- espy [v.] -- to see sb/sth suddenly or unexpectedly, at a long distance

12 -- etch [v.] -- *(a).* to produce a line, mark, pattern or design into a piece of hard material such as glass, metal, etc. using sharp material or acid [*synonym*: scrape] | ***(b).*** (of a feeling) to be clearly seen on sb's face | ***(c).*** to make a strong clear line, mark, pattern or design on sth

13 -- evil [adj.] -- *(a).* (of people) morally wrong, bad, unkind and cruel, and enjoying harming others | ***(b).*** having a harmful effect on people that is considered morally wrong or bad | ***(c).*** connected with the Devil and with what is considered morally wrong or bad | ***(d).*** extremely unpleasant || **[n.] -- *(a).*** morally wrong, bad, unkind and cruel behavior that causes harmful effects | ***(b).*** a wrong, bad or harmful thing; the bad or harmful effect of sth

4-Letter Words -- F

01 -- fade [v.] -- *(a).* to become or to make sth become less bright, strong or fresh, in a gradual manner | *(b).* to disappear in a gradual manner from sight, hearing, memory, etc | *(c).* (of a sports player, team, performer, etc.) to stop playing or performing as well as before

02 -- fain (adv.) -- willingly or happily || **[adj.]** -- compelled by the circumstances or willing/happy under the circumstances

03 -- fake [adj.] -- *(a).* not true, real or genuine; appearing to be sth while actually, it is not [*synonyms*: counterfeit, forged, fraudulent, sham] | *(b).* made to look or seem like sth else [*synonym*: imitation] || **[n.]** -- *(a).* an object such as a coin, currency note, portrait or a piece of jewelry, etc. that is not genuine but has been made to look as if it is [*synonyms*: forgery, sham] | *(b).* a person who acts as if he/his sb else in order to cheat people || **[v.]** -- *(a).* to make sth false appear to be real or genuine, so you can cheat sb | *(b).* to act as if you have a particular feeling, emotion, illness, etc.

04 -- fame [n.] -- the state of being widely known and much talked about by a lot of people because of your achievements [*synonym*: renown]

05 -- fang [n.] -- *(a).* two long sharp or pointed teeth of a venomous snake used to inject poison | *(b).* a large sharp or pointed canine tooth of a dog or wolf | *(c).* the mouthpart of a spider that is used to bite

06 -- faux [adj.] -- not real, but intended to look or seem real [*synonyms*: artificial, fake, false]

07 -- fawn [adj.] -- of light yellowish-brown in color [*synonym*: beige] || **[n.] -- (a).** a light yellowish-brown color [*synonym*: beige] | **(b).** a young deer, especially one that is less than one year old || **[v.]** -- to try to please or get the approval of sb by giving them a lot of attention or by praising them highly in an insincere way [*synonym*: flatter, grovel]

08 -- faze [v.] -- [often passive] to make you feel confused, surprised, worried, disturbed and shocked [*synonym*: disconcert]

09 -- feat [n.] -- an action or achievement that needs great courage, skill, or strength

10 -- feud [v.] -- to have an angry and bitter argument, disagreement, quarrel or dispute with sb for a prolonged period of time || **[n.]** -- an angry and bitter argument, disagreement, quarrel or dispute between two people or groups of people for a prolonged period of time [*synonym*: row]

11 -- fiat [n.] -- an authoritative, legal or official order given by sb in authority [*synonym*: decree]

12 -- fizz [n.] -- (a). the bubbles in a liquid and the sound they make | **(b).** cheerfulness, excitement, or liveliness || **[v.] -- (a).** (of a liquid) to produce a lot of bubbles and make a hissing sound [*synonyms*: effervesce, froth] | **(b).** to show cheerfulness, excitement, or liveliness

13 -- flab [n.] -- soft, loose, extra flesh on a person's or an animal's body [*synonym*: fat]

14 -- flaw [n.] -- (a). a small mistake in sth that shows it does not or cannot work correctly or perfectly [*synonyms*: defect, fault] | **(b).** a crack, mark or fault in an object that reduces its attraction, beauty, value or perfection [*synonym*: blemish] | *(c).* a weakness in sb's character [*synonym*: failing]

15 -- **flay** [v.] -- *(a).* to remove the skin from a dead animal or person | *(b).* to hit or whip sb so harshly and violently that some of their skin comes off | *(c).* to remove the outer covering of sth | *(d).* to criticize sb/yourself severely

16 -- **flee** [v.] -- to run away from a place very quickly, especially because you are afraid of possible danger [*synonym*: escape]

17 -- **flex** [v.] -- to bend, move or stretch a part of your, especially in order to prepare for an exercise or physical activity | [n.] -- (a piece of) the wire inside a plastic tube, used for carrying electricity to electrical equipment

18 -- **flit** [v.] -- to fly, move or pass lightly and quickly from place to place [*synonym*: flutter]

19 -- **flog** [v.] -- *(a).* [often passive] to punish sb by hitting or beating them hard several times with a whip, stick or rod | *(b).* to sell sth to sb

20 -- **flop** [v.] -- *(a).* to sit or lie down in a heavy, noisy and sudden way because of tiredness [*synonyms*: slump, collapse] | *(b).* to fall, move, drop or hang in a heavy, loose, awkward or uncontrolled manner [*synonym*: droop] | *(c).* to be a total failure || [n.] -- an unsuccessful movie, play or party, etc.

21 -- **flub** [v.] -- to do sth badly or poorly; or to make a mistake when performing sth [*synonyms*: botch, bungle, fluff] || [n.] -- a thing that is done badly or poorly [*synonyms*: botch, bungle, fluff]

22 -- flux [n.] -- *(a).* condition of a series of continuous movements and changes | *(b).* the action or process of flowing ions, body fluid, etc.

23 -- foal [n.] -- a very young horse, donkey or mule || **[v.] --** (of a mare) to give birth to a foal (a very young horse, donkey or mule)

24 -- ford [v.] -- to walk or drive across a river or stream at a shallow place || **[n.] --** a shallow place in a river where it is possible to cross safely by walking on foot or driving a vehicle

25 -- free [adj.] -- *(a).* able to do or say what you want without being influenced or restricted by the control or power of sb else | *(b).* (of a person) not a captive, prisoner, hostage, slave, etc. | *(c).* not attached or tied with string, rope, etc.; not trapped by sth, or not being in a cage or similar structure that restricts your movement | *(d).* that can be got without paying anything; without charge | *(e).* having without a thing that can block the way; clear | *(f).* not containing or affected by sth harmful or unpleasant | *(g).* being remained unused | *(h).* (of a person or time) not having anything to do; not having particular arrangements || **[v.] --** *(a).* to let sb leave a place such as a prison, cage or enclosure they have been kept against their will [*synonym*: release] | *(b).* to move sb/sth that is caught, fixed, stuck, trapped or on sth | *(c).* to remove the unpleasant or unwanted thing from sb/sth [*synonym*: rid] | *(d).* to make sb/sth available for a particular task, function or purpose | *(e).* to give sb the additional time to perform a particular task, function || **[adv.] --** *(a).* without charge or payment | *(b).* away from or out of a place/position in which sb/sth is caught, stuck or trapped; without being controlled, restricted or stopped

26 -- fret [v.] -- to be worried, dissatisfied, uncomfortable or unhappy [*synonym*: fuss]

27 -- fume [v.] -- *(a).* to feel, show, or express great anger about sth | ***(b).*** to produce smoke, gas or vapor

28 -- funk [v.] -- to avoid doing sth out of fear or because you find it difficult || **[n.] -- *(a).*** a strong unpleasant smell | ***(b).*** a state of fear or worry or nervousness

29 -- fury [n.] -- *(a).* extreme, violent and wild anger and passion about sth [*synonyms*: rage, wrath] | ***(b).*** a state of showing extreme, violent and wild anger and passion about sth [*synonym*: rage] | ***(c).*** effect of strong floods, storms, wind and other climatic events

30 -- fuss [v.] -- *(a).* to do unimportant or unnecessary things, or pay too much attention to unimportant or unnecessary things | ***(b).*** to worry about unimportant or unnecessary || **[n.] -- *(a).*** needless activity, excitement, worry, nervousness | ***(b).*** anger, complaints or criticisms about sth unimportant

31 -- fuzz [n.] -- *(a).* short soft fine hair or fur that covers a person's face or arms [*synonym*: fluff] | ***(b).*** a mass of hair in tight curls | ***(c).*** sth, that is not easy to see clearly | ***(d).*** the fuzz *(slang)* -- the police

4-Letter Words -- G

01 -- **gaff** [n.] -- *(a).* a stick or pole with a hook or barbed spear used to pull large fish out of the water | *(b). (slang)* -- the house, flat / apartment, etc. to live for sb

02 -- **gait** [n.] -- a way of walking [*synonym*: pace]

03 -- **gale** [n.] -- *(a).* an extremely strong wind | *(b).* a sudden and loud expression of emotions in the form of laughter, tears, etc.

04 -- **gall** [n.] -- *(a).* extremely rude, impolite, disrespectful and shameless behavior [*synonyms*: effrontery, impudence] | *(b).* a long-lasting bitter feeling that is full of extreme dislike [*synonyms*: hatred, resentment] | *(c).* a swelling on the external tissues of plants, trees, fungi, or animals caused by insects, disease, etc. || [v.] -- to make sb feel angry, upset and distressed, especially because sth is not fair or reasonable [*synonyms*: infuriate, vex]

05 -- **gape** [v.] -- *(a).* to look at sb/sth with an open mouth because of anger, shock or surprised | *(b).* to be or become wide open || [n.] -- *(a).* an act of looking at sb/sth with an open mouth because of anger, shock or surprised | *(b).* a state of becoming wide open

06 -- **garb** [n.] -- unusual or special kind of clothes, worn by a particular type of person [*synonyms*: attire, costume]

07 -- **gash** [v.] -- to make a long deep cut or wound on the surface of a person's skin [*synonym*: slash] || [n.] -- a long deep cut or wound on the surface of a person's skin [*synonym*: slash]

08 -- gasp [v.] -- (a). to take a short, quick, sudden, deep and noisy breath with the mouth open, especially because of excitement, shock, surprise or pain | **(b).** to have difficulty breathing or speaking || **[n.] --** a short, quick, sudden, deep and noisy breath, usually caused by excitement, shock, surprise or pain

09 -- gawk [v.] -- to openly, rudely or stupidly look at sb/sth for a long time [*synonym*: gape] || **[n.] --** an awkward, graceless tactless or shy person

10 -- gawp [v.] -- to openly, rudely or stupidly look at sb/sth for a long time [*synonym*: gawk]

11 -- gaze [v.] -- to fix your eyes at sb/sth with concentration for a long period of time, because they are interesting, admiring, or curious, etc. or because you are thinking of sth else [*synonym*: stare] || **[n.] --** a steady look at sb/sth for a long period time

12 -- gear [n.] -- (a). (in a vehicle) a rotating circular machine that turns engine power into movement forwards or backward | **(b).** (in a vehicle) a particular position of the gears to give a specific range of power and speed | **(c).** items that sb owns or possesses | **(d).** clothes or garments | **(e).** the equipment or clothing that is needed for a particular purpose or activity | **(f).** effort or speed involved in doing sth | **(h).** (slang) -- illegal drugs

13 -- geek [n.] -- (a). a boring and unfashionable person who does not know behave properly in social situations, etc. [*synonym*: nerd] | **(b).** a person who is extremely interested in computers or other technological fields

14 -- gist [n.] -- the main or general meaning or point of a piece of information, text, speech, conversation or literary work [*synonyms*: essence, substance]

15 -- glee [n.] -- a feeling of happiness or excitement, usually because of one's own good fortune or another's misfortune or trouble. [*synonyms*: delight, merriment]

16 -- glen [n.] -- a deep narrow valley among mountains especially in Scotland

17 -- glib [adj.] -- (of words or the speakers) clever and voluble but insincere and not showing serious thoughts or feelings [*synonym*: persuasive]

18 -- glob [n.] -- a round-shaped small amount of a semi-liquid substance

19 -- glop [n.] -- thick, sticky and formless substance that is unpleasant to taste or feel [synonyms: gunk, goo, slime]

20 -- glug [v.] -- *(a).* (of liquid) to pour out quickly while making a gurgling sound, especially from a bottle | *(b).* to drink sth quickly || **[n.] --** a small amount of liquid poured out; a gurgling sound made by a small amount of liquid poured out

21 -- glum [adj.] -- disappointed, quiet and sad [*synonym*: gloomy]

22 -- glut [v.] -- to provide sth so much that supply exceeds demand || **[n.] --** a situation in which sth is much more than requirement [*synonyms*: excess, surfeit. surplus]

23 -- **gnaw [v.]** -- *(a).* to keep biting, cutting or chewing on sth with teeth repeatedly, until it completely disappears or destroys [*synonym*: nibble] | *(b).* to make sb feel nervous, worried or terrified over a long period of time

24 -- **goad [v.]** -- to irritate, upset or annoy sb/sth continuously until they react or do sth || **[n.]** -- *(a).* a pointed stick or other instrument used for making an animal move forwards | *(b).* sth that makes sb react or do sth, usually by irritating, upsetting or annoying them

25 -- **gory [n.]** -- *(a).* full of blood or violence | *(b).* covered with blood [*synonym*: bloodstained]

26 -- **grim [adj.]** -- *(a).* (of a person) looking or sounding very serious and sad; not smiling | *(b).* (of a situation, news, etc.) unpleasant, worrying and disappointing *(c).* (of a place or building) unattractive and unpleasant [*synonym*: depressing] | *(d).* [not usually before noun] of not up to the mark; of very low or poor quality | *(e).* [not before noun] ill/sick

27 -- **grin [v.]** -- to smile widely, revealing a lot of teeth || **[n.]** -- a wide smile that reveals a lot of teeth

28 -- **grub [n.]** -- *(a).* larva, the young form of an insect, that looks like a small fat worm | *(b).* hearty food || **[v.]** -- to look for sth, by digging or by looking through or under the soil, etc.

29 -- **guff [n.]** -- silly ideas

30 -- **gulp [v.]** -- *(a).* to swallow large amounts of food, drink, air, etc. hurriedly, eagerly or greedily | *(b).* to make a swallowing movement, especially because of a strong emotion such as fear, worry or surprise | *(c).*

to breathe quickly, deeply and audibly, because of the need of more air || **[n.]** -- *(a).* an amount of food, drink, air, etc. that you swallow hurriedly, eagerly or greedily | *(b).* an act of breathing in or of swallowing food, drink, air, etc

31 -- gust [n.] -- *(a).* a sudden, strong wind that blows for a very short period of time | *(b).* a sudden and unexpected rush or burst of rain, wind, water, fire, smoke, sound, etc. | *(c).* a sudden strong expression of particular emotion or feeling | **[v.]** -- (of the wind) to suddenly blow in a very hard manner

4-Letter Words -- H

01 -- halo [n.] -- *(a).* a circle of light shown around or above the head of a holy/religious person or thing to show their holiness, in a drawing or painting [*synonym*: aura] | *(b).* a ring of light that surrounds the sun, moon or other heavenly bodies

02 -- halt [v.] -- to stop or make sb/sth stop moving, operating, happening or doing sth, either permanently or temporarily || [n.] -- a short stop in some activity, progress, movement or growth; an act of stopping activity, progress, movement or growth

03 -- haze [n.] -- *(a).* a mixture of smoke, dust, fine sand and light water vapor, especially caused by hot weather, that fills the air and makes it difficult to see through [*synonym*: mist] | *(b).* air containing sth that reduces its visibility | *(c).* a mental state in which you cannot think in a clear way or feel about sth in a normal way

04 -- hazy [adj.] -- *(a).* (of air) not clear because of haze [*synonyms*: foggy, misty] | *(b).* unclear owing to a lack of detail, facts, memory or understanding [*synonym*: vague] | *(c).* (of a person) confused and not certain about sth [*synonym*: muddled]

05 -- heap [v.] -- *(a).* to place, throw, or lay a large group of things one on another in an unorganized manner | *(b).* to put a lot of sth in an unorganized manner on sth | *(c).* to give a lot of praise, criticism, etc. to sb || [n.] -- *(a).* a large group of things or objects placed, thrown, or lying one

on another in an unorganized manner [*synonyms*: mound, pile] | *(b).* a lot of sth [*synonym*: plenty]

06 -- heed [v.] -- to pay close and careful attention to sth esp. advice or warning [*synonym*: observe]

07 -- heir [n.] -- *(a).* a person who has the legal right to receive sb's property, money, rank or title after the death of the owner | *(b).* a person who continues the work, custom or a tradition that else started [*synonyms*: successor, inheritor]

08 -- hike [v.] -- *(a).* to go for a long walk in the country, woods, etc., especially for pleasure [*synonym*: trek] | *(b).* to increase prices, costs, taxes, etc. suddenly or by large amounts | **[n.]** -- *(a).* a long walk in the countryside, woods, etc. especially for pleasure [*synonym*: trek] | *(b).* a large, sudden or unwanted and increase in prices, costs, taxes, etc. of sth

09 -- hilt [n.] -- the handle of a sword, knife, etc.

10 -- hoax [n.] -- an act or a plan that is designed to make sb or a group of people accept or believe sth that is false and absurd, especially sth unpleasant [*synonym*: trick] || **[v.]** -- to trick sb or a group of people by making them accept or believe sth that is false and absurd, especially sth unpleasant

11 -- holy [adj.] -- *(a).* [usually before noun] relating to God or a particular religion and therefore very important or special [*synonym*: sacred] | *(b).* morally or religious way good; pure | *(c).* [only before noun] used to emphasize surprise, anxiety, fear, etc.

12 -- hone [v.] -- *(a).* to develop and improve a skill or talent, over a period of time: [*synonym*: polish] | *(b).* : to make an object such as a blade sharp or smooth with a whetstone [*synonym*: sharpen]

13 -- honk [n.] -- *(a).* the noise made by a goose | *(b).* the noise made by a car horn || **[v.] --** *(a).* (of a car horn) to make a loud noise [*synonym*: hoot] | *(b).* (of a goose) to make a loud noise

14 -- hood [n.] -- *(a).* a part of a coat, cloak, etc. that covers the neck and top of your head | *(b).* a piece of cloth that completely covers sb's face and head in order to hide their identity or so that they cannot see | *(c).* a piece of colored silk or fur worn over an academic gown to show the kind of degree held by the person wearing it | *(d).* a folding cover over a car, byke, etc.; a cover placed over a machine, to protect, hide, etc. it | *(e).* the movable covering for the engine of an automobile; bonnet | *(f).* (*slang*) a violent criminal, especially a member of a street gang | *(g).* (*slang*) a person's own neighborhood

15 -- huff [v.] -- *(a).* to say sth or make a noise in an annoying way or in a manner that shows you are angry or offended [*synonym*: sulk] | *(b).* to breathe loudly, quickly or heavily, because of physical exercise [*synonyms*: gasp, puff] || **[n.] --** a state of irritation or annoyance

16 -- huge [adj.] -- *(a).* extremely large, big or great in amount, size or degree [*synonyms*: enormous, extensive, vast] | *(b).* extremely successful

17 -- hulk [n.] -- *(a).* the main part of an old, dismantled and unused ship or any other vehicle | *(b).* a very large and heavy person who moves awkwardly | *(c).* a very large, heavy and awkward-looking object that makes you feel nervous or afraid

18 -- hull [v.] -- to remove the shell or husk (outer covering) of beans, peas, grains, etc. or the stem and leaves attached to fruits, vegetables, and seeds || **[n.] --** the main body of a ship, boat, etc. including the bottom part and sides that floats on the water

19 -- hurl [v.] -- *(a).* to throw sth/sb with a great force in a particular direction [*synonyms*: chuck, toss] | *(b).* to say sth forcefully, especially to shout accusations, insults, etc. at sb || *(b). (slang)* to vomit

20 -- hush [v.] -- *(a).* (used in orders) to be silent or quiet; to stop talking, chattering, crying, etc. | *(b).* to make sb/sth become silent or quieter; to make sb stop talking, chattering, crying, etc. || **[n.] --** a period of silence, following a lot of noisy activity, or when sth is expected to be going to happen

21 -- husk [n.] -- the dry outer covering of grain, seeds, nuts, fruits, etc. [*synonym*: shell] || **[v.] --** to remove the dry outer covering of grain, seeds, nuts, fruits, etc.

22 -- hype [v.] -- to advertise, promote or publicize sth such as a product or idea a lot on television, social media, newspaper, etc. in order to attract intensive public attention often overstating its advantages || **[n.] --** excessive advertisement, promotion or discussion relating to a product or idea on television, social media, newspaper, etc. in order to attract intensive public attention often overstating its advantages

4-Letter Words -- I

01 -- iced [adj.] -- *(a).* (of drinks) made extremely cold; containing pieces of ice [*synonyms*: frozen, refrigerated] | *(b).* (of a cake, biscuit, etc.) covered or decorated with icing.

02 -- idle [v.] -- *(a).* to spend time in a meaningless way or without doing anything | *(b).* (of an engine) to run at a slow speed while the vehicle is not moving [*synonym*: tick over] | *(c).* to temporarily close a factory, company, etc. or stop providing work for the staff or workers || **[adj.]** -- *(a).* (of people) not working hard or nor wanting to work hard [*synonyms*: lazy, lethargic] | *(b).* (of machines, factories, etc.) not being used; not working or functioning [*synonyms*: inactive, inoperative] | *(c).* (of people) not doing any work or job for livelihood [*synonym*: unemployed] | *(d).* [usually before noun] having no particular purpose, use or effect [*synonym*: redundant] | *(e).* [usually before noun] (of time) not spent doing anything important

03 -- idly [adv.] -- without any particular or real basis, reason, purpose or effort; doing nothing; in an idle manner [*synonyms*: aimlessly, lethargically]

04 -- idol [n.] -- *(a).* a person or thing that is admired, loved and respected very much [*synonym*: icon] | *(b).* a statue or other object that is worshipped as a god

05 -- iffy [adj.] -- *(a).* not in perfect condition, state or form | *(b).* uncertain, doubtful or undecided

06 -- inch [v.] -- to move or make sth move carefully, slowly, and gradually in a particular direction [*synonym*: creep] **|| [n.] -- *(a).*** a unit for measuring length, equal to 2.54 centimeters or one-twelfth of a foot **|** *(b).* a small amount or distance

07 -- inky [adj.] -- *(a).* as black or dark as ink [*synonym:* pitch-black] **|** *(b).* made dirty with ink

08 -- iota [n.] -- *(a).* (usually used in negative sentences) an extremely small or tiny amount of sth [*synonyms*: jot, whit] **|** *(b).* the 9th letter (I, ι) of the Greek alphabet

09 -- itch [v.] -- *(a).* to have an irritating or uncomfortable feeling or sensation on your skin that causes a desire to rub or scratch it hard; to make your skin feel like this **|** *(b).* (often used in the progressive tenses) to have a very strong desire to do sth very much **|| [n.] --** *(a).* an irritating or uncomfortable feeling or sensation on your skin that causes a desire to rub or scratch it hard **|** *(b).* a very strong desire to do sth

4-Letter Words -- J

01 -- **jeer** [*v.*] -- to laugh at sb/sth, or shout insulting, unkind or rude remarks at them to show that you don't respect or like them [*synonyms*: ridicule, taunt]

02 -- **jest** [*n.*] -- sth false or non-serious that is said or done to make sb amuse or laugh [*synonym*: joke] || [*v.*] -- to say false or non-serious things, especially in order to make sb amuse or laugh [*synonym*: tease]

03 -- **jibe** [*n.*] -- an unkind, insulting or embarrassing remark about sb [*synonym*: taunt] || [*v.*] -- *(a).* to say sth that with an intention to embarrass sb | *(b).* to be in the agreement with sth or to match it

04 -- **jilt** [*v.*] -- [often passive] to end a romantic relationship with sb in suddenly and unkindly; to break up with

05 -- **jink** [*v.*] -- to move quickly, irregularly and suddenly, especially in order to avoid sb/sth

06 -- **jinx** [*n.*] -- *(a).* bad luck | *(b).* a person or thing that brings bad luck || [*v.*] to bring bad luck to sb/sth [*synonym*: curse]

07 -- **jolt** [*v.*] -- *(a).* to move/push or to make sb/sth move/push suddenly, violently and roughly | *(b).* to give sb a sudden surprising shock to make them start to take action to deal with a particular situation [*synonym*: shake] || [*n.*] -- *(a).* a sudden, strong, rough and violent movement | *(b).* a sudden strong feeling of shock or surprise

08 -- **josh** [*v.*] -- to make fun of sb playfully or talk to them jokingly [*synonym*: tease]

09 -- **jowl** [*n.*] -- the fold of loose skin and flesh under the chin and jaws

4-Letter Words -- K

01 -- keel [v.] -- (of a ship or boat) to fall over sideways; to make sth fall over sideways [*synonym*: capsize] || **[n.] --** a long piece of timber or metal extending along the entire length of the bottom of a boat or ship that stops it from falling over sideways in the water

02 -- kick [v.] -- *(a).* to hit or strike sb/sth, especially forcefully, with your foot [*synonym*: boot] | *(b).* to move your legs as if you were hitting or striking sth | *(c).* (kick yourself) to be angry or upset with yourself because you have missed an opportunity, done sth silly/wrong, etc. | *(d).* (in football and rugby) to score points by hitting or striking the ball || **[n.] --** *(a).* a sudden forceful movement that is made with your foot or the leg, usually to hit sth | *(b).* a very strong feeling of pleasure and excitement | *(c).* the strong effect that an alcoholic drink or a drug has

03 -- kiln [n.] -- a large oven for burning, baking or drying clay, bricks, etc. [*synonym*: furnace]

04 -- kink [v.] -- to develop or make sth develop a sharp bend, twist or curve || **[n.] --** *(a).* a sharp bend, twist or curve in sth that is usually in straight line | *(b).* an unusual and abnormal feature in a person's character or mind

05 -- kohl [n.] -- a black powder or substance that is put along the edges of sb's eyelids to make them more attractive

06 -- kook [n.] -- a person who acts or behaves strangely or crazily

4-Letter Words -- L

01 -- lack [v.] -- [no passive] to not have sth or not enough of sth that is needed, desired or wanted || **[n.]** -- the fact, state or condition of not having sth or not having enough of sth that is needed, desired or wanted [*synonyms*: dearth, shortage]

02 -- lady [n.] -- *(a).* a polite, well-behaved, well-spoken and well-educated woman | *(b).* a polite word for "woman" used especially for an adult female | *(c).* an informal and somewhat insulting way to talk to a woman | *(d).* the female head of a household | *(e).* a woman who belongs to a good family or high social class/position | *(f).* (a / the ladies or 'ladies' room) public toilet/bathroom for women | *(g).* a woman, sometimes highly skilled, who is in the position of authority | *(h).* used to talk to or talk about an unknown girl or woman

03 -- lair [n.] -- *(a).* a place for a wild animal to sleep, live, rest or hide | *(b).* a place where a person goes to rest, hide or be alone [*synonyms*: den, hideout]

04 -- lame [adj.] -- *(a).* (of people or animals) unable to walk properly because of an injury or disability to the leg or foot | *(b).* (of an excuse, argument, explanation, etc.) weak and difficult to be believed [*synonyms*: feeble, unconvincing]

05 -- lash [v] -- *(a).* (of wind, rain and storms) to hit sb/sth forcefully [*synonym*: pound] | *(b).* to hit a person or an animal forcefully and violently with a whip, rope, stick, etc. [*synonym*: beat] | *(c).* to criticize sb/sth severely or angrily | *(d).* to tie or fasten sth tightly or firmly to sth else with ropes [*synonym*: fasten] | *(e).* to move side to side in a sudden, quick and violent manner; to move sth suddenly, quickly and violently from side to side || **[n.]** -- a hit with a whip, rope, stick, etc.

06 -- laud [v.] -- to praise sb/sth highly [*synonyms*: acclaim, extol]

07 -- laze [v.] -- to spend time in a relaxed, idle or lazy manner enjoying yourself, doing very little or no work || **[n.]** -- a short period of time of lazing around

08 -- lean [v.] -- *(a).* to be in a sloping position; to bend, lean or move from a vertical position into a sloping position | *(b).* to rest against sth for support such as a wall, etc.; to make sth rest against sth in a leaning or sloping position || **[adj.]** -- *(a).* [usually before noun] (of a period of time) difficult and unproductive | *(b).* (of edible meat) having little or no fat | *(c).* (of organizations, etc.) strong and efficient because in the reduction of the number of employees | *(d).* (of people or animals) without much flesh or fat; fit and thin || **[n.]** -- the part of edible meat that has little or no fat

09 -- leap [v.] -- *(a).* to jump high or over a long distance [*synonym*: dive] | *(b).* to move or do sth in a sudden and quick manner | *(c).* to increase in a sudden way and by a large amount [*synonym*: soar] || **[n.]** -- *(a).* a long, big or high jump | *(b).* a sudden large change or increase in sth

10 -- leer [v.] -- to look or smile at sb in an unpleasant and offensive way with wicked intention towards sb || **[n.]** -- an unpleasant or offensive look or smile that shows wicked intention towards sb

11 -- levy [n.] -- an extra amount of payment, tax, etc. **| [v.] --** to officially demand and collect a payment, tax, etc.

12 -- lewd [adj.] -- (of behavior, dress, speech, etc.) referring to sex in a rude, obvious and offensive manner [*synonyms*: obscene, vulgar]

13 -- lick [v.] -- *(a).* to move or pass your tongue across or over sth to eat, taste, or clean it, or make it wet **|** *(b).* to eat or drink sth by moving or passing your tongue across or over it **|** *(c).* (of flames) to touch sth in a light manner **|| [n.] --** an act of moving or passing your tongue across or over sth to eat, taste, or clean it, or make it wet

14 -- lien [n.] -- the right to keep possession of sb's property, etc. until a debt owed by that person is paid

15 -- lilt [n.] -- *(a).* a gentle and pleasant rise and fall of a person's voice **|** *(b).* a regular rise and fall in music, with a strong rhythm

16 -- limb [n.] -- *(a).* an arm or a leg of a person or an animal; a wing of the bird **|** *(b).* a large branch of a tree

17 -- limp [v.] -- *(a).* to walk slowly, irregularly, awkwardly or with difficulty because one leg or foot is injured **|** *(b).* to move slowly, irregularly, awkwardly or with difficulty after being damaged **|| [adj.] --** *(a).* deficient in strength or energy **|** *(b).* stiff, firm or strong **|| [n.] --** a way of walking wherein one leg or foot is used less than normal because of injury or stiffness

18 -- lode [n.] -- a line of metal ore in the earth or rocks

19 -- loll [v.] -- *(a).* to lie, sit or stand in a lazy, relaxed way or position without doing much at all [*synonyms*: lounge, slouch] | ***(b).*** (of the head or other part of the body.) to move or hang loosely | ***(c).*** (of sb's tongue) to stick out and hang loosely; to stick out and hang your tongue to loosely

20 -- lone [adj.] -- *(a).* without any companion, friend or other people or things [*synonym*: solitary] | ***(b).*** without a husband, wife or partner [*synonym*: single] | ***(c).*** standing by itself or apart [*synonym*: isolated]

21 -- loom [v.] -- *(a).* to appear as an unclear large shape that seems frightening or threatening | ***(b).*** to appear important, frightening or threatening and likely to occur soon

22 -- lope [v.] -- to run with long steps || **[n.] --** a run with long steps

23 -- lore [n.] -- *(a).* traditional and popular knowledge, intelligence, teachings and information about a particular subject, that is not written down but passed down orally from one person to person, especially from older people to younger ones | ***(b).*** the stories, traditions or set of beliefs of a particular group of people

24 -- lout [n.] -- rude and aggressive boy or man [*synonym*: yob]

25 -- lull [v.] -- *(a).* to make sb feel calm, relaxed, sleepy, confident or safe [*synonym*: soothe] | ***(b).*** to make sth less strong; to become less strong | **[n.] --** a short quiet, calm period in a longer period of activity

26 -- lump [v.] -- to put or consider different things collectively in the same group || **[n.] -- *(a).*** a piece of sth hard or solid, usually without a definite or regular shape | ***(b).*** a hard swelling in the body, especially under the skin, that may be the sign of serious illness or injury | *(c).* a heavy, lazy or dim-witted person

28 -- **lure [v.]** -- to attract a person or animal and make them do sth or go somewhere by offering or promising them a reward [*synonyms*: entice, tempt] || **[n.]** -- *(a).* the attractive qualities of sth | *(b).* an object that is used to attract fish or wild animals to catch them

28 -- **lurk [v.]** -- *(a).* to wait or move somewhere quietly and secretly to avoid being seen, with an intention to do sth bad, evil or illegal [*synonyms*: prowl, skulk] | *(b).* (of sth unpleasant or dangerous) to be present but not in a clear or understandable way

29 -- **lush [adj.]** -- *(a).* (of plants, gardens, etc.) growing thickly, strongly and attractively; covered in healthy grass and plants [*synonym*: luxuriant] | *(b).* (esp. of fruits) juicy and fleshy | *(c).* beautiful and making you feel pleasure; seeming expensive

4-Letter Words -- M

01 -- mace [n.] -- *(a).* a decorative stick, carried by an official as a sign or symbol of authority | *(b).* a large heavy stick with sharp-pointed metal parts on the top, that was used as an armor-breaking weapon in the past [*synonym*: club] | *(c).* an aromatic spice made of the dried outer covering of nutmeg (= a type of hard nut)

02 -- maim [v.] -- to injure or wound a person or animal severely, causing permanent damage to the part of their body [*synonyms*: disfigure, incapacitate]

03 -- mane [n.] -- *(a).* long and heavy hair growing on the neck and head of horses, lions and some other mammals | *(b).* long heavy hair on a person's head. [*synonym*: locks]

04 -- mart [n.] -- a trade center where goods are bought and sold

05 -- maul [v.] -- *(a).* (of wild animal) to attack and injure sb by tearing their flesh [*synonym*: savage] | *(b).* to criticize sth/sb harshly and publicly [*synonym*: savage] | *(c).* to touch sb/sth in an unpleasant, rough and violent way | *(d).* to defeat sb without difficulty || **[n.] --** a heavy long-handled hammer

06 -- meek [adj.] -- (of people) quiet, kind, and always willing to do what other people say or want to do without asking questions or expressing your opinions [*synonyms*: submissive, shy] || **[n.] --** (the meek) people who are quiet, kind, and always willing to do what other people say or want to do without asking questions or expressing your opinions

07 -- mega -- [adj.] -- very large, great and impressive [*synonym*: huge]

08 -- meld [v.] -- to combine with sth else in a pleasant or useful way; to make sth combine with sth else in a pleasant or useful way [*synonym*: blend]

09 -- mewl [v.] -- *(a).* (especially of a baby or young child) to make a weak, soft, high crying sound [*synonym*: whimper] | *(b).* (of a cat or bird) to make a weak, soft, high-pitched crying noise [*synonym*: mew]

10 -- mien [n.] -- a person's general appearance, manner, etc. or typical expression on their face, as showing character, feeling, mood, etc.:

11 -- mild [adj.] -- *(a).* (of illness, injury, etc.) not severe, violent or strong | *(b).* (of weather) pleasantly cold or fairly warm | *(c).* (of a flavor) not strong, harsh or spicy | *(d).* (of feelings) not great or extreme [*synonym*: slight] | *(e).* (of people, their behavior or way of speaking) gentle, calm, kind and polite [*synonyms*: equable, humble]

12 -- mint -- [v.] -- to make coins from metal, especially for use as currency | **[n.]** -- *(a).* a large amount of money | *(b).* to make coins from metal, especially for use as currency

13 -- moan [v.] -- *(a).* (of a person) to make a long deep sound, because of unhappiness, pain, suffering, or physical pleasure [*synonyms*: groan, whimper] | *(b).* to keep complaining about sth unimportant in an annoying way [*synonyms*: grumble, whine] | *(c).* (of the wind) to make a long deep sound || **[n.]** -- *(a).* a long deep sound, expressing unhappiness, pain, suffering, or physical pleasure [*synonym*: groan] | *(b).* a complaint about sth | *(c).* a long deep sound, that is made by the wind

14 -- mock [v.] -- *(a).* to copy what sb/sth say or do and laugh at them in an unkind way | *(b).* to show no respect or value for sth || **[adj.] --** *(a).* [only before noun] not sincere or truthful | *(b).* that is a copy of sth; unreal || **[n.] --** a practice exam before the real or official one

15 -- moll [n.] -- the female friend or companion of a criminal

16 -- monk [n.] -- a member of a religious group of men who gives up pleasures of worldly life and lives in a monastery (a building in which monks live and worship)

17 -- moor [v.] -- to attach or tie up a boat, ship, etc. to a fixed object on land or to the surface under the water, with a rope or chain [*synonym*: fasten] || **[n.] --** *(a).* a high open area of land with poor soil covered with rough grass and heather (a type of a wild plant), not used for farming | *(b).* land that is composed of moors

18 -- moot [v.] -- [usually passive] to suggest an idea or possibility, or raise a question or topic to discuss publicly || **[adj.] --** *(a).* impractical, insignificant, doubtful and unlikely to happen and therefore not worth considering | *(b).* subject to argument, debate, dispute, or uncertainty. [*synonym*: debatable]

19 -- mope [v.] -- to feel apathetic, dejected, unhappy and unwilling to think or act in a positive manner because of disappointment about sth [*synonyms*: brood, sulk, languish]

20 -- mote [n.] -- a very small or tiny piece of dust, dirt, etc. [*synonym*: speck]

21 -- **muck [n.]** -- *(a).* waste matter from farm animals or rotting vegetables, plants, etc. that is used to make living plants grow better [*synonym*: manure] | *(b).* wet dirt or mud [*synonym*: slime] | *(c).* a very unpleasant sticky substance

22 -- **murk [n.]** -- darkness or dimness caused by smoke, fog, etc. [*synonym*: gloom]

23 -- **muse [v.]** -- *(a).* to think carefully about sth for a long time and deeply without caring what is happening around you [*synonym*: ponder] | *(b).* to say sth (often with writing at the same time) to yourself in a way that shows you are absorbed in a careful thought || **[n.]** -- *(a).* a person or spirit who is the object of devotion or love and gives sb such a writer, painter, etc. an inspiration to create things | *(b).* (Muse) (in ancient Greek and Roman mythology) each of the nine goddesses, the daughters of Zeus and Mnemosyne who governs music, poetry and other activities relating to art, literature and science

24 -- **muss [v.]** -- to make sb's clothes or hair untidy or messy

25 -- **mute [adj.]** -- *(a).* not speaking; absence of speech | *(b).* (of a person) unable or unwilling to speak; [*synonyms*: speechless, voiceless] | *(c).* (of an activity, object, or a place) silent || **[v.]** -- *(a).* to make the sound of a musical instrument, quieter or softer | *(b).* to make sth weaker or less severe

26 -- **myth [n.]** -- *(a).* a traditional well-known story that explains the historical event or person [*synonym*: legend] | *(b).* an idea, story, etc. that is believed by many people but that is not true or does not exist [*synonym*: fallacy]

4-Letter Words -- N

01 -- naff [adj.] -- not stylish, lacking quality or taste [*synonym*: unfashionable]

02 -- nape [n.] -- the back of the neck

03 -- nark [n.] -- (*slang*) a person who makes friendly relations with criminals or wrongdoers to give the police information about their activities [*synonyms*: informer, spy]

04 -- nerd [n.] -- *(a).* a boring, foolish, introverted and unfashionable person [*synonym*: geek] | ***(b).*** a person who is too much interested in computers || **[v.] --** to obsessively engage in or discuss a technical field

05 -- nick [n.] -- *(a).* a small cut, slit, damage or hollow place in the edge or surface of sth [*synonyms*: notch, scratch] | ***(b).*** (the nick) a prison or a police station | ***(c).*** (*slang*) (the nick) a prison or a police station || **[v.] -- *(a).*** to make a small cut, slit, damage or hollow place in the edge or surface of sth | ***(b).*** to catch and arrest sb for committing a crime | ***(c).*** to go somewhere fast and sudden way | ***(d).*** to steal sth, especially sth small and not very valuable [*synonym*: pinch]

06 -- nigh [adv.] -- *(a).* almost; nearly | ***(b).*** at a short distance away [*synonym*: near] || **[adj.] --** located or situated a short distance away || **[prep.] --** at or to a short distance away

07 -- nook [n.] -- a small quiet sheltered or hidden place or corner

08 -- **nosh [n.]** -- *(a).* a small amount of food that is eaten quickly between main meals | *(b). (slang)* food; a meal || *[v.]* -- to eat food in an enthusiastic or greedy way

09 -- **nuke [n.]** -- a nuclear bomb or other nuclear weapons || *[v.]* -- to attack a place with a nuclear bomb or other nuclear weapons

10 -- **null [adj.]** -- *(a).* having the value zero [*synonyms*: nil, worthless] | *(b).* that has no effect

4-Letter Words -- O

01 -- oath [n.] -- a formal, sincere and ritualistic promise to do sth or a formal, sincere or ritualistic statement that sth is true based on an appeal to some revered person, object, god or God [*synonym*: pledge]

02 -- obey [v.] -- *(a).* to do what you are expected to do based on rules or principles | ***(b).*** to act according to the command, instruction, wish, etc. of sb else

03 -- ogre [n.] -- *(a).* (in stories) a cruel, fierce, and frightening man-eating giant | ***(b).*** a very cruel, frightening person that causes a problem for sb

04 -- omen [n.] -- a sign or an event that tells what evil or good is going to happen in the future [*synonym*: portent]

05 -- omit [v.] -- to exclude or leave out sth/sb, either intentionally or because you have forgotten it/them

06 -- onus [n.] -- the responsibility or duty for sth

07 -- ooze [v.] -- *(a).* (of a thick liquid) to move, flow or leak slowly out of a particular place; to allow a thick liquid to move, flow or leak slowly out of a particular place [*synonym*: seep] | ***(b).*** to strongly show a particular characteristic, quality, etc. [*synonym*: exude] || **[n.] -- *(a).*** very soft mud, at the bottom of a water body such as a lake, river or sea | ***(b).*** the very slow flow of a thick liquid

08 -- oozy [adj.] -- *(a).* with moisture or thick liquid coming out of sth | ***(b).*** full of very soft mud

09 -- oral [adj.] -- *(a).* [usually before noun] spoken or uttered by the mouth rather than written [*synonym*: verbal] | *(b).* [only before noun] connected with the mouth; within or into the mouth [*synonym*: vocal] | *(c).* (of a speech sound) produced by the flow of air through the mouth but not the nose || **[n.] --** a spoken exam or test, in a university or in a foreign language

10 -- ours [pron.] -- that which belongs to us; relating to the person who is speaking and to one or more other people

11 -- oust [v.] -- to cause or force sb to leave the position of power, a job, place, or competition, especially in order to take their place

4-Letter Words -- P

01 -- pact [n.] -- a formal agreement or contract between two or more people, groups or countries [*synonym*: concord]

02 -- pacy [adj.] -- *(a).* (of a book, film/movie, etc.) having a story that moves, develops or progresses quickly | *(b).* able to run quickly [*synonym*: fast]

03 -- pale [adj.] -- *(a).* (of a person, or their face, etc.) having skin that is almost white or whiter than usual because of illness or a strong emotion such as fear, shock, embarrassment, etc. [*synonym*: whitish] | *(b).* (of light) less strong or bright than usual | *(c).* (of color) containing a lot of white; light | *(d).* lacking in brilliance, intelligence, importance, etc. || **[v.]** -- *(a).* (of a person, or their complexion) to become whiter than usual because of illness or a strong emotion such as fear, embarrassment, etc. | *(b).* (of light) to become less strong or bright than usual | *(c).* (of color) to have a lot of white | *(d).* to be less brilliant, intelligent, important, etc. than usual

04 -- pall [v.] -- (not used in the progressive tenses) to lose strength or effectiveness over a period of time and become boring [*synonyms*: diminish, fade, wither] || **[n.]** -- *(a).* a thick dark cloud of smoke, dust, etc. | *(b).* a cloth covering spread over a coffin, hearse, or tomb during the funeral ceremony

05 -- pane [n.] -- a single flat piece or sheet of glass in a window or door

06 -- pang [n.] -- a sudden, sharp and strong feeling of physical or emotional distress or pain [*synonym*: twinge]

07 -- pare [v.] -- *(a).* to cut away the thin outer layer of sth [*synonym*: peel] | *(b).* to cut away the edges of sth such as your nails to make them neat and smooth | *(c).* to reduce the size or amount in a gradual manner

08 -- pave [v.] -- [often passive] to cover a surface of the road, ground, etc. with flat stones, asphalt, concrete or bricks

09 -- peal [n.] -- *(a).* a loud, deep sound or series of sounds | *(b).* the loud, deep, prolonged ringing sound of a bell | *(c).* a set of bells that all have different notes || **[v.]** -- (of bells) to make a loud, deep prolonged sound [*synonym*: clang]

10 -- peck [v.] -- *(a).* (of birds) to quickly move the beak forward and hit, pick or bite sth | *(b).* to hit sth quickly with a pointed or sharp instrument or object | *(b).* to kiss sb lightly and quickly, especially on the side of the face || **[n.]** -- *(a).* (of birds) an act of quickly moving the beak forward and hitting, picking or biting sth | *(b).* an act of hitting sth quickly with a pointed or sharp instrument or object | *(c).* a light and quick kiss, especially on the side of the face

11 -- peek [v.] -- to look quickly and secretly at sth that you are not supposed to look at || **[n.]** -- a quick and secret look at sth

12 -- peel [v.] -- *(a).* to take the skin off a fruit, vegetable, etc. | *(b).* to remove a natural layer, covering, shell, etc. slowly and carefully from the surface of sth | *(c).* (of a covering, layer or shell) to come off in strips or small/narrow pieces | *(d).* (of a surface) to lose strips or small/narrow pieces of its covering, layer or shell || [n.] -- the thick skin or covering of some fruits and vegetables [*synonym*: rind]

13 -- peep [v.] -- *(a).* to look quickly, slightly, playfully or secretly at sth, especially through a small opening or from a hidden location [*synonym*: glance] | *(b).* to make a short, high-pitched sound or noise; to cause sth to make short, high-pitched sound or noise [*synonyms*: chirp, twitter] | *(c).* to be just able to be seen || **[n.] --** *(a).* a quick, slight, playful or secret look at sth, especially through a small opening or from a hidden location [*synonym*: glance] | *(b).* sth that is said by sb; a sound that is made by sb | *(c).* a short, high-pitched sound or noise, as made by a whistle or young bird noise [*synonyms*: chirp, twitter]

14 -- peer [v.] -- to look closely or carefully at sth, especially sth that is not easy or clear to see [*synonym*: gaze] || **[n.] --** a person of the same age, background, social/legal status, or having the same abilities/qualifications as other people in a group or level

15 -- pelt [v.] -- *(a).* to attack sb by throwing a number of things quickly at them [*synonym*: shower] | *(b).* (of rain) to fall very heavily | *(c).* to move or run somewhere with great speed [*synonym*: dash] || **[n.] --** animal's skin and fur or hair

16 -- perk [n.] -- benefits that sb receives besides the wages for doing a particular job [*synonym*: perquisite]

17 -- pest [n.] -- *(a).* an insect that attacks and destroys the food, plant, livestock, etc. [synonym: bug] | *(b).* a person or thing that causes annoyance [synonym: nuisance]

18 -- **plea** [n.] -- *(a).* an urgent emotional and serious request [*synonym*: appeal] | *(b).* a statement made by sb, especially who is accused of a crime | *(c).* a reason or rationale given to a court for doing or not doing sth

19 -- **plod** [v.] -- *(a).* to walk slowly with heavy steps in a tiring way [*synonyms*: lumber, trudge] | *(b).* to make slow progress in a boring and difficult way

20 -- **plop** [n.] -- a sound like that of an object falling or dropping into water || [v.] -- *(a).* to fall, making a plop | *(b).* to drop sth into water or other liquid so that it makes a sound; to drop, fall or move with a sound like that of an object falling or dropping into water | *(c).* to sit or lie down heavily or without taking care; to put sth down heavily or without taking care

21 -- **pill** [n.] -- *(a).* a small piece of medicine in the form of a ball, tablet or capsule that is swallowed whole by the patient without chewing it | *(b).* anything unpleasant that cannot be avoided

22 -- **ping** [v.] -- *(a).* to make a short, high ringing or musical sound; to make sth produce this sound | *(b).* to send a text message, especially to sb's mobile phone || [n.] -- a short, high ringing or musical sound made when a small bell or other hard object hits sth made of glass or metal

23 -- **pity** [n.] -- *(a).* a strong feeling of sympathy and sadness caused by the suffering, troubles, misfortunes or difficult situations of others [*synonym*: mercy] | *(b).* used to show your disappointment about sth [*synonym*: shame] || [v.] -- (not used in the progressive tenses) to feel sorry for sb because of their suffering, troubles, misfortunes or difficult situations

24 -- ploy [n.] -- a cunning action, plan or word carefully planned or designed to get an advantage over sb else [*synonym*: maneuver (manoeuvre)]

25 -- plum [adj.] -- (of a job, post, position, etc.) very good and worth having || **[n.]** -- *(a).* a soft, round, fleshy fruit with red, purple or yellow skin and a large flat seed inside in the middle; a plum tree | *(b).* a dark reddish-purple color

26 -- poky [adj.] -- *(a).* (of a room or a building) too or uncomfortably small that has not much space [*synonym*: cramped] | *(b).* moving or acting slowly or ineffectively that causes annoyance

27 -- pomp [n.] -- traditional customs with special or impressive clothes, decorations, music, etc. that are part of an official or formal occasion or ceremony

28 -- pong [n.] -- a strong unpleasant smell || **[v.]** -- to give out a strong unpleasant smell

29 -- pony [n.] -- *(a).* type of small horse, usually not over 58 inches | *(b).* (slang) £25 | *(c).* (slang) a small measure of alcohol || **[v.]** -- to pay a sum of money, as a contribution or unavoidable expense

30 -- pore [n.] -- *(a).* one of the very small holes in the skin of people or other animals | *(b).* one of the very small holes in the surface of a plant or a rock || [*synonym*: aperture]

31 -- posy [n.] -- a small bunch of flowers [*synonym*: bouquet]

32 -- prod [v.] -- *(a).* to push sb/sth quickly with your finger or with an object that has a pointed end | *(b).* to try to encourage or remind sb to do sth, against their willingness || **[n.] --** *(a).* the act of pushing sb with your finger or with a pointed object [*synonym*: dig] | *(b).* the act of trying to encourage or remind sb to do sth, against their willingness

33 -- puke [v.] -- to eject the contents that you have eaten or drunk through the mouth [*synonym*: vomit]

34 -- purl [n.] -- a stitch used in knitting || **[v.] --** to make a stitch in knitting

35 -- pyre [n.] -- a large pile of wood along with other combustible substances on which a dead body is placed and burned as part of a funeral rite

4-Letter Words -- Q

01 -- quip [v.] -- to make a quick and clever remark to a comment [*synonyms*: retort] **|| [n.] --** a quick and clever remark [*synonym*: witticism]

02 -- quit [v.] -- *(a).* to permanently leave your job, educational institute, etc. **|** *(b).* to permanently leave the place of your residence **|** *(c).* to stop having, using, or doing sth [*synonym*: relinquish] **|** *(d).* to close and stop using a computer program or application

03 -- quiz [n.] -- *(a).* a competition or game for entertainment purposes between individuals or teams to test their knowledge through questions and answers **|** *(b).* an informal test or examination that is given to students in the form of questions **|| [v.] --** *(a).* to ask sb a series of questions about sth to get information from them [*synonym*: question] **|** *(b).* to give students an informal test

4-Letter Words -- R

01 -- rage [n.] -- *(a).* a feeling of very strong, uncontrolled and violent anger [*synonym*: fury] | *(b).* very strong, uncontrolled and violent anger caused by a particular situation || **[v.] --** *(a).* to express your intense anger about sth or with sb by shouting [*synonym*: rail] | *(b).* (of an argument, a storm or a war, etc.) to keep on continuing in a violent way or with great intensity | *(c).* (of an illness, a fire, etc.) to spread at a very fast speed causing immense damage | *(d).* (slang) to go out and do things you enjoy

02 -- ramp [n.] -- a slop that is used or formed to connect two parts of sth such as a path, building, etc. when one is higher than another

03 -- rant [v.] -- to speak, shout or complain about sth in a loud, uncontrolled, noisy, excited or angry way for a long time [*synonyms*: fume, seethe]

04 -- rapt [adj.] -- deeply interested in, fascinated by or paying careful attention to one particular thing you are seeing or hearing and therefore not aware of anything else [*synonyms*: captivated, engrossed, immersed]

05 -- rare [adj.] -- *(a).* not done, seen, found, occurring, etc. very often[*synonyms*: exceptional, infrequent, scarce] | *(b).* existing only in limited number or quantity, or not having of many kinds, and therefore valuable or interesting | *(c).* (of meat) cooked very lightly so that the inside is still red

06 -- rash [adj.] -- (of people or their actions) acting or done insensibly, without careful consideration about the possible results [*synonyms*: impetuous, impulsive, reckless] || **[n.]** -- *(a).* an area of a lot of small red spots, patches, bumps that appear on a person's skin due to an illness or an allergic or bad reaction to sth [*synonyms*: itchiness, pimples] | *(b).* a lot of or series of unpleasant things or unfortunate events occurring over a short period of time [*synonym*: spate]

07 -- rasp [v.] -- *(a).* to say sth in a rough, harsh, unpleasant voice | *(b).* to make a rough unpleasant sound [*synonym*: grate] | *(c).* to rub a rough surface with a rasp (long-bladed and rough-surfaced metal tool) or with a rasp-like rough object || **[n.]** -- *(a).* a rough, harsh, unpleasant sound | *(b).* a long-bladed and rough-surfaced metal tool or similar tools that are used for making rough surfaces of metal, wood, or other hard material smooth through rubbing

08 -- rave [v.] -- *(a).* to talk or write about sth enthusiastically | *(b).* to shout in a loud, angry and emotional way at sb [*synonym*: rant] | *(c).* to talk or shout in an illogical or insensible manner [*synonym*: ramble] || **[n.]** -- a large party where there is a lot of dancing activity at fast electronic music and at which people often take illegal drugs

09 -- raze [v.] -- [usually passive] to destroy sth such as a building, town, etc. completely so that nothing is left [*synonyms*: annihilate, demolish]

10 -- ream [v.] -- to treat sb in an unfair manner; to cheat them || **[n.]** -- *(a).* (reams) a large amount of written or printed information | *(b).* 500 sheets of paper

11 -- **reap** [v.] -- *(a).* to obtain sth as a direct result of your deeds | *(b).* to cut and collect wheat or other crops from a field [*synonym*: harvest]

12 -- **rely** [v.] -- *(a).* to depend on sb/sth, or to need support, supply, or help, etc. to continue, to work correctly, or to achieve your goal | *(b).* to trust or have full faith/confidence in sb/sth

13 -- **rife** [adj.] -- *(a).* of sth bad, undesirable or unpleasant) very common or frequent [*synonym*: widespread] | *(b).* full of sth bad or unpleasant || [adv.] -- in a widespread manner

14 -- **rift** [n.] -- *(a).* a serious disagreement between friends, groups, etc. that breaks their relationship [*synonyms*: breach, division] | *(b).* a very large crack or opening in the ground, rocks or clouds [*synonyms*: cleft, chink, fissure]

15 -- **rile** [v.] -- to make sb very angry or annoyed [*synonym*: enrage]

16 -- **rind** [n.] -- the thick tough outer skin of some types of fruits or foods such as lemon, orange, etc.; the coating on cheese or bacon

17 -- **roam** [v.] -- *(a).* to walk, go or travel around an area without any definite or particular purpose, direction or plan [*synonym*: wander] | *(b).* (of the eyes or hands) to move slowly over each and every part of sb/sth

18 -- **roar** [v.] -- *(a).* (of lion, tiger or some other wild animals) to make a very deep, long, loud sound [*synonym*: growl] | *(b).* (of a person) to shout sth loudly due to excitement, pain, distress, or anger [*synonym*: yell] | *(c).* (of a fire) to burn with a lot of flames, heat, brightness and noise | *(d).* (of a vehicle) to move at high speed, making a lot of noise | *(e).* to laugh in a

very loud manner || **[n.]** -- *(a).* a deep, long, loud sound made by a lion tiger or some other wild animals | *(b).* a deep, long, loud sound by a person due to excitement, pain, distress, or anger | *(c).* a loud continuous noise made by the sea, wind, or by a machine

19 -- robe [n.] -- a long loose-fitting outer garment reaching to the ankles, especially one worn in a very formal or special ceremony occasion || **[v.]** -- [usually passive] to dress sb/yourself in the long loose-fitting outer garment

20 -- romp [v.] -- to play happily and noisily || **[n.]** -- easily achieved victory in a sports competition

21 -- root [n.] -- *(a).* the part of a plant that attaches it to the ground and absorbs water and minerals, that are used by the rest of the plant | *(b).* the part of a hair, nail, tooth or tongue that attaches it to the rest of the body | *(c).* (roots) the particular place you or your old generations belonged to and the connections, feelings or experiences you or your old generations have had living there | *(d).* the main or basic cause, source, or origin of a problem, difficult situation, etc.; the origin or basis of sth | *(e).* a base word, or a part of a word to which suffixes or/and affixes are added | *(f).* a quantity which produces another quantity, on multiplication by itself a particular number of times || **[v.]** *(a).* to grow roots; to make a plant or cutting to grow roots | *(b).* to establish deeply and firmly | *(c).* to move things around carelessly, unsystematically or untidily while searching for sth [*synonym*: rummage] | *(d).* (slang) to make a physical relationship with sb

22 -- rosy [adj.] -- *(a).* (of person's skin, cheeks, lips, etc.) having a fresh, healthy, pleasant redness; colored like a red or pink rose | *(b).* likely to be good or successful [*synonyms*: optimistic, promising]

23 -- rote [n.] -- the process of learning a fact, etc. by repetition rather than by understanding or paying attention to the meaning of it

24 -- rout [v.] -- to defeat your opponent completely in a competition, a battle, etc. || **[n.]** -- the complete and easy defeat of your opponent in a battle or competition

25 -- rove [v.] -- *(a).* to aimlessly travel from one place to another [*synonym*: roam] | *(b).* (of sb's eyes) to keep looking in different directions || **[n.]** -- a journey without any specific destination; an act of travel without any aim

26 -- ruin [v.] -- *(a).* to damage or destruct a building, place, etc. severely or badly in such a way it loses all its value, etc [*synonyms*: spoil, wreck] | *(b).* to make sb/sth lose all their money, possession or power || **[n.]** -- *(a).* the state or process of being severely or badly damaged or destructed | *(b).* the fact of having no job, money, possession or power | *(c).* sth that causes a person, company, etc. to completely lose their job, money, possession or power [*synonym*: downfall] | *(d).* (also ruins) the parts of a building or place that remain after it after severe damage or destruction

27 -- ruse [n.] -- a way of doing sth or of getting sth in a dishonest manner [*synonym*: trick]

28 -- rush [v.] -- *(a).* to move or to do sth too fast because of urgency | *(b).* to send or transport sb/sth somewhere with extremely fast speed | *(c).* to do sth thoughtlessly and carelessly or to make sb do sth thoughtlessly and carelessly | *(d).* to try to suddenly attack or capture sb/sth | *(e).* (in American Colleges) to give a lot of attention to a student in order to make them join your group | *(f).* (in American football) to run towards the opposition player who has carrying a ball | (of a player) to move the ball by running with it || **[n.] --** *(a).* a sudden strong fast and forward movement of people, air, water, etc. | *(b).* a situation in which there is a lot of activity and people are very busy | *(c).* a sudden strong emotion; a sudden feeling of excitement, happiness, pleasure, etc; a sudden feeling of extreme pleasure or excitement especially after taking some types of drugs | *(d).* (the rush) the period of time of heavy traffic on roads | *(e).* a situation in which you are in a hurry because of lack of time and need to do things quickly | *(f).* a sudden large demand for products, etc. | *(g).* a grass-like tall plant that grows in water | *(h).* (in American Colleges) the time when parties are held for students who want to join your group | *(i).* (in American football) an occasion when a player/players run towards the opposition player who has carrying a ball; an occasion when a player moves the ball by running with it

4-Letter Words -- S

01 -- **saga [n.]** -- *(a).* a long, detailed, traditional story about adventures and brave acts | *(b).* a long, detailed, complicated story that spans over a period of many years | *(c).* a long, detailed, complicated series of events or adventures || [*synonyms*: chronicle, legend]

02 -- **sage [adj.]** -- wise and knowledgeable, because of having a lot of experience [*synonym*: learned] || **[n.]** -- a very wise and knowledgeable person

03 -- **sane [adj.]** -- *(a).* having a normal healthy mind and not mentally ill or crazy | *(b).* sensible, reasonable and showing good judgment

04 -- **sans [prep.]** – without

05 -- **sass [n.]** -- rude and insulting behavior or talk | **[v.]** -- to speak to sb in a rude and insulting way

06 -- **sate [v.]** -- to satisfy a desire [*synonym*: quench]

07 -- **scam [n.]** -- a clever, deceptive, dishonest plan for making money [*synonym*: fiddle]

08 -- **scar [v.]** -- *(a).* (of a wound, injury, etc.) to leave a mark that is caused by a cut, burn or sore, on the skin after it has healed | *(b).* (of an unpleasant experience) to leave sb with a long-lasting feeling of great sadness, mental pain or other negative effects | *(c).* to spoil spoils the look or public image of sth || **[n.]** -- *(a).* a mark that is caused by a cut, burn or sore, and is left on the skin after a wound has healed | *(b).* a long-lasting

feeling of great sadness, mental pain or other negative effects after an unpleasant experience | *(c).* an unpleasant or ugly thing that spoils the look or public image of sth | *(d).* an area of a hill or cliff where there is the rock that has no, trees, plants or grass

09 -- scud [v.] -- (of clouds) to move quickly across the sky

10 -- scum [n.] -- *(a).* a layer of unwanted/dirty/unpleasant substance, often in the form of bubbles on the surface of a liquid or water body [*synonym*: froth] | *(b).* an insulting word for people that you strongly dislike

11 -- sear [v.] -- *(a).* to suddenly and powerfully burn the surface of sth [*synonym*: singe] | *(b).* to cause sb to feel sudden strong pain

12 -- seep [v.] -- (of liquids) to flow, pass, move, or spread slowly and in small quantities through sth or into sth which is porous [*synonym*: trickle]

13 -- seer [n.] -- a person who has the power to see or predict the future [*synonym*: prophet]

14 -- shin [n.] -- the front part of the leg below the knee to the foot

15 -- shun [v.] -- to avoid sb/sth [*synonyms*: eschew, shirt]

16 -- sift [v.] -- *(a).* to pass flour, sugar, ash or other fine substance through a sieve | *(b).* to examine sth very carefully to find important or useful things | *(c).* to separate sth from a group of things

17 -- silt [n.] -- clay, sand, soil or mud, etc. that is carried by flowing water and is collected at the sides or on the bottom of a pond, river and other water bodies [*synonym*: sediment]

18 -- skew [v.] -- *(a).* to change, influence or distort sth in a way that is inaccurate, unfair, abnormal, misleading. etc. | *(b).* to suddenly move or lie in a position or direction that is not normal || **[n.] -- *(a).*** a tilted position or direction; not straight [*synonym*: slant] | *(b).* partiality towards a particular group or subject || **[adj.] --** neither parallel or even nor at right angles to a particular line; [*synonyms*: askew, crooked]

19 -- skid [v.] -- (especially of a vehicle) to uncontrollably slide sideways or forwards || **[n.] --** the movement of a vehicle when it uncontrollably and suddenly slides sideways

20 -- slab [n.] -- *(a).* a thick, large, flat, broad piece of stone, wood or other hard and solid material | *(b).* a thick, flat, broad slice or piece of sth such as bread

21 -- slag [n.] -- *(a).* the stony and glass-like waste material left over after metal has been removed during refining of its raw ore | *(b).* (slang) an insulting term for a woman, used to indicate that she has a lot of partners for having physical relations || **[v.] --** to produce the stony and glass-like waste material left over after metal has been removed during refining of its raw ore

22 -- slam [v.] -- *(a).* to shut, or to make sth shut, very forcefully and loudly [*synonym*: bang] | *(b).* to put, push or throw sth somewhere quickly and very forcefully | *(c).* to hit a vehicle or object, causing damage; to make a vehicle or object do this | *(d).* (used especially in newspapers) to criticize sb/sth in a very strong or harsh manner || **[n.] --** an act of slamming sth; the sudden loud noise of sth being slammed

23 -- slay [v.] -- to kill sb/sth violently, especially in a war or a fight

24 -- slew [v.] -- (especially of a vehicle) to turn or slide suddenly and awkwardly in another direction; to make a vehicle do this [*synonym*: skid] || **[n.]** -- a large number, amount or quantity of sth

25 -- slim [adj.] -- *(a).* thinner than usual or normal | *(b).* (of chance, margin and other abstract things) very small in comparison with what you would like or expect [*synonym*: small] | *(c).* (of a person or their build) attractively thin || **[v.]** -- (usually used in the progressive tenses) to try to become thinner, especially by dieting || **[n.]** -- a course or period of slimming

26 -- slit [v.] -- to make a long, narrow, straight cut or opening in sth || **[n.]** -- a long, narrow, straight cut or opening

27 -- slob [n.] -- a lazy and dirty or untidy person

28 -- slog [v.] -- *(a).* to work hard and steadily at sth, over a long period of time, that is boring or difficult | *(b).* to go, walk or travel gradually and in an even and regular way, with great effort or difficulty [*synonyms*: plod, trudge] | *(c).* (in cricket) to hit a ball forcefully and uncontrollably without much skill | (in boxing) to hit the opponent forcefully and typically wildly || **[n.]** -- *(a).* a period of hard and tiring work, effort or traveling | *(b).* (in cricket) a forceful and uncontrolled hit

29 -- smog [n.] -- dirty, poisonous or harmful air that is a mixture of smoke, gases, and chemicals that often covers a whole city

30 -- smug [adj.] -- looking or feeling too much pleased, satisfied or proud with yourself, your abilities or achievements [*synonyms*: conceited, snobbish]

31 -- snip [n.] -- *(a).* an act of cutting or clipping sth with scissors using short quick strokes; the sound that is produced by this action | *(b).* (a snip) a cheap and good-valued thing

32 -- snip [v.] -- to cut or clip sth with scissors using short quick strokes [*synonym*: shear]

33 -- snob [n.] -- *(a).* a person who is a great admirer of people belonging to higher social classes and criticizes disrespects or ignores people belonging to the lower social classes | *(b).* a person who thinks or feels they are better, more intelligent, more important, more superior, etc. than other people

34 -- snub [v.] -- *(a).* to treat sb with contempt, disrespect or neglect, especially by refusing to look at or speak to him/her when you meet [*synonym*: cold-shoulder] | *(b).* to refuse to attend or accept sth [*synonym*: boycott] || **[adj.]** -- [only before noun] (of a nose) flat, short and turned up at the end || **[n.]** -- an action or a comment that is deliberately rude to show contempt or disrespect for sb [*synonym*: insult]

35 -- snug [adj.] -- *(a).* warm, comfortable and protected from cold weather [*synonym*: cozy] | *(b).* fitting sb/sth closely | **[n.]** -- a small comfortable room in a pub or inn with limited seats

36 -- soar [v.] -- *(a).* (of the value, amount or level) to rise very speedily [*synonym*: rocket] | *(b).* to rapidly and smoothly rise high up into the air |

(c). to fly or remain very high in the air | *(d).* to become very high or tall | *(e).* (of music) to become higher or louder

37 -- sole [adj.] -- [only before noun] *(a).* being the only one [*synonyms*: only, single, solitary] | *(b).* acting, working, etc. alone without the help of others | *(c).* (responsibility, duty, right, ownership, etc) belonging to one person or group; that is not shared with others || **[n.] --** *(a).* the bottom surface of the foot | *(b).* the part of a shoe or sock that covers the bottom surface of your foot | *(c).* a type of flat sea fish that is used for food || **[v.] --** [usually passive] to repair a shoe by replacing the sole (= the part of a shoe or sock that covers the bottom surface of your foot)

38 -- soot [n.] -- black powder, mostly consisting of carbon, that is produced when wood, coal, etc. is burnt

39 -- spat [n.] -- a short argument, disagreement or quarrel about sth unimportant [*synonym*: row]

40 -- spew [v.] -- *(a).* to flow out quickly and forcefully, or to make sth flow out quickly and forcefully, in large amounts | *(b).* to bring food from the stomach back out involuntarily through the mouth [*synonym*: vomit]

41 -- spud [n.] -- a potato

42 -- stab [v.] -- *(a).* to kill or injure sb by pushing a knife or other sharp, pointed object, tool or weapon into them | *(b).* to make a short, aggressive or violent movement with a finger or sharp, pointed object, tool or weapon [*synonyms*: jab, prod] || **[n.] --** *(a).* an act of killing or injuring sb by pushing a knife or other sharp, pointed object, tool or weapon into them | *(b).* an injury or wound that was caused by a knife or other sharp, pointed object, tool or weapon | *(c).* a sudden sharp strong pain or unpleasant feeling

43 -- stag [n.] -- a male deer

44 -- stew [v.] -- *(a).* to cook food slowly, or allow food to cook slowly, in liquid for a long time in a closed container [*synonym*: simmer] | *(b).* to be restless, worried or upset about sth || **[n.] --** a dish of meat and/or vegetables cooked in liquid for a long time in a closed container

45 -- stow [v.] -- to put sth in a safe or hidden place

46 -- suck [v.] -- *(a).* to pull in liquid or air into your mouth by using the lips | *(b).* to hold sth in your mouth and pull on it by contracting your lips, tongue or cheek muscles | *(c).* to forcefully draw sth in a particular direction | *(d).* to take the air, liquid, etc. out of sth | *(e).* (*slang*) (sth sucks) used to say that you dislike sth very much because it is of extremely bad quality, taste, etc. or filled with boredom, terrible situation, etc. || **[n.] --** *(a).* an act of pulling in liquid or air into your mouth by using the lips | *(b).* an act of holding sth in your mouth and pulling on it by contracting your lips, tongue or cheek muscles | *(c).* an act of forcefully drawing sth in a particular direction | *(d).* an act of taking air, liquid, etc. out of sth

47 -- suds [n.] -- a mass of very small bubbles that forms on the surface of soapy water [*synonym*: lather]

48 -- swap [v.] -- *(a).* to give sth to sb and receive sth else in return [*synonyms*: barter, exchange, trade] | *(b).* to remove sb/sth and put another person or thing in their place | *(c).* to begin to do sb else's work, job, duty, etc. while they do yours | **[n.] --** *(a).* an act of giving sth to sb and receiving sth else in return | *(b).* a thing or person that has been replaced or exchanged for another

49 -- swat [v.] -- to hit sth hard, especially an insect with the hand or a flat object [*synonyms*: swipe, whack] | **[n.]** - an act of hitting sth hard with the hand or a flat object [*synonyms*: swipe, whack]

50 -- sway [v.] -- *(a).* to move slowly and gently from side to side, or back and forth; to move sth in this way | *(b).* [often passive] to make sb believe sth. agree with sth or do sth [*synonym*: influence] || **[n.] --** *(a).* a slow and gentle movement from side to side, or back and forth | *(b).* power, control or influence over sb

4-Letter Words -- T

01 -- **tack** **[n.]** -- the ability to skillfully, sensitively and adeptly deal with the difficult situation

02 -- **tact** **[n.]** -- the ability and skill to deal with difficult or embarrassing situations or issues carefully and sensitively to avoid upsetting or offending other people [*synonym*: discretion]

03 -- **tame** **[adj.]** -- *(a).* (of animals, birds, and other creatures) not afraid of people, and used to living near or with them; changed from a wild to a domesticated state | *(b).* not interesting, lively or exciting [*synonym*: boring] | *(c).* (of a person) willing to do what is asked by other people [*synonyms*: docile, meek, submissive] || **[v.]** -- to bring sth wild under your control

04 -- **tamp** **[v.]** -- to press sth down firmly into a closed space, by hitting it several times in a light manner

05 -- **tang** **[n.]** -- a strong and distinctive sharp taste, smell or flavor

06 -- **tart** **[adj.]** -- *(a).* (especially of fruit) having a sharp sour taste | *(b).* [usually before noun] (of remarks, etc.) quick, harsh and unkind || **[n.]** -- a shallow pastry case filled with sweet food and no top crust

07 -- **task** **[v.]** -- [usually passive] to assign a piece of work, especially a hard or unpleasant one that sb has to do or undertake || **[n.]** -- *(a).* a piece of work, especially a hard or unpleasant but important one that sb has to do or undertake, often regularly or unwillingly and typically as part of a larger

project [*synonyms*: assignment, chore] | *(b).* an activity designed to help achieve a particular learning goal

08 -- taut [adj.] -- *(a).* stretched or pulled very tightly [*synonym*: rigid] | *(b).* (of a person or their body) lean with firm muscles | *(c).* showing that you are nervous, worried, angry or tense | *(d).* (of a piece of writing, music, etc.) tightly controlled, without having unnecessary parts in it

09 -- teem [v.] -- (usually be teeming) (of rain) to fall heavily or a lot

10 -- thud [v.] -- *(a).* to move, fall, or hit sth with a low, dull, heavy sound | *(b).* (especially of the heart) to beat strongly [*synonym*: thump] | **[n.] --** a low, dull, heavy sound, like the one which is produced when a heavy solid object falls to the ground or hits sth else [*synonym*: thump]

11 -- thug [n.] -- a violent criminal

12 -- thus [adv.] -- *(a).* in this or that way; like this or that | *(b).* as a result of this or of sth just mentioned [*synonyms*: hence, therefore]

13 -- tiff [n.] -- a small, unimportant or petty argument, fight or quarrel between close friends, etc. [*synonym*: squabble]

14 -- toil [v.] -- *(a).* to work very hard continually, usually doing hard physical work | *(b).* to move slowly in a particular direction with great difficulty or effort [*synonym*: slog] || **[n.] --** hard unpleasant physical work that is very tiring

15 -- tome [n.] -- a large, heavy and scholarly book that deals with a serious topic

16 -- tosh [adj.] *(slang)* -- nonsense [*synonym*: rubbish]

17 -- trap [n.] -- *(a).* a piece of equipment or enclosure that are designed for catching and retaining animals | *(b).* a clever plan or situation designed to trick sb into doing or saying sth; **a** clever plan or situation designed to attack sb to kill them or trick sb to capture them | *(c).* a very unpleasant situation, often horrific one, that is hard to escape from | *(d).* an enclosure through which a greyhound (= a particular kind of dog) is let out at the beginning of a race | *(e).* a strongly built underground shelter for soldiers or guns | *(f).* a light horse-carriage with two wheels | *(g). (slang)* mouth [*synonym*: gob] || **[v.] --** *(a).* to keep sb in a dangerous place or horrific situation that they can't escape from | *(b).* to have part of your body, clothing, objects, etc. held tightly in a particular place in such a way that it can't be removed easily and may suffer injury or damage | *(c).* to catch and keep sth in a place so that they can't escape and you can use them later | *(d).* to trick sb/sth into a particular place or situation in order to catch them | *(e).* to catch an animal in a trap (a piece of equipment or enclosure) | *(f).* to trick sb into doing or saying sth

18 -- trio [n.] -- *(a).* a set or group of three people or things that have sth in common | *(b).* a set or group of three musicians or singers who play or sing together | *(c).* a composition (a piece of music) for three musicians or singers

19 -- trip [n.] -- *(a).* a short journey, for pleasure or a particular purpose, to a particular place and back again, [*synonym*: excursion] | *(b).* an act of falling or nearly falling down, because you catch your foot against sth or hit your foot on sth [*synonym*: stumble] | *(c). (slang)* the experience of seeing or hearing things that are not really there that sb has if they are under the influence of a powerful drug (psychoactive substances) || **[v.]** -- *(a).* to catch your foot on sth and fall down or almost fall down; to catch sb's foot and make them fall down or almost fall down [*synonym*: stumble] | *(b).* to walk, run or dance with quick light steps | *(c).* to operate sth by releasing a switch, etc.; to release a switch, etc. | *(d).* to be under the influence of a powerful drug (psychoactive substances) that affects your mind and makes you see or hear things that are not really there

20 -- tuft [n.] -- a number of short pieces of hair, feathers, grass, threads. etc. growing, attached or held together at the base [*synonyms*: bunch, clump]

21 -- twee [adj.] -- appearing very attractive, pretty, or too perfect to be real, in a way that seems unpleasant and silly; appearing sentimental

22 -- twig [v.] -- to understand or realize sth suddenly || **[n.] --** a small thin branch on a tree, plant or bush

23 -- tyro [n.] -- a person without much or any experience of an activity, or is a beginner in learning about an activity [*synonym*: novice]

4-Letter Words -- U

01 -- ugly [adj.] -- *(a).* unpleasant in appearance or to look at [*synonym*: unattractive] | *(b).* (of an event, a situation, etc.) unpleasant, dangerous, threatening or violent

02 -- undo [v.] -- *(a).* to open sth that is closed fastened, tied or wrapped | *(b).* to cancel or reverse the effect or result of an action | *(c).* [usually passive] to make sb/sth fail

03 -- unit [n.] -- *(a).* a single or individual thing, person, number, group, etc. that is a component of a whole but can also become or form part of sth larger | *(b).* a group of people working or living together to achieve a particular goal or for a particular purpose | *(c).* one of the parts into which a school course, textbook or a series of lessons is divided to focus on a particular theme or topic | *(d).* a fixed quantity, as of length, time, heat, etc. that is used as a standard measurement | *(e).* a cupboard or other piece of furniture, that fits with and matches others of the same or similar kind | *(f).* a department in a medical facility, that is equipped to provide a particular type of care or treatment | *(g).* a part of a military establishment with a set organization | *(h).* a small machine or apparatus that performs a particular function or is part of a larger machine or apparatus | *(i).* a single flat/apartment in a building; a group of buildings containing a number of flats/apartments | *(j).* any whole number from 0 to 9; the number one, the first and least natural number | *(k).* a small molecule when combined in a larger molecule | *(l).* a particular amount of an antigen, drug or other biologically active agents that are required to produce a particular result | *(m).* a single item of the type of product that is being sold by a company

04 -- urge [v.] -- *(a).* to advise or encourage sb very strongly to do sth | *(b).* to suggest, propose or recommend sth strongly | *(c).* to force, drive or push a person or an animal to move or go more quickly and/or in a particular direction || **[n.]** -- a strong need or desire to do sth

05 -- user [n.] -- *(a).* a person or thing that uses or operates sth such as a product, machine, facility or service, etc. | *(b).* (law) the continued enjoyment or use of a right | *(c).* (slang) a person who uses drugs that are illegal

4-Letter Words -- V

01 -- **vamp** [n.] -- a woman who is extremely attractive in a physical way and who tries to control men

02 -- **vary** [v.] -- *(a).* (of a group of similar things) to be different from each other in amount, appearance, character, form, level, shape, size, substance, etc. [*synonym*: differ] | *(b).* to change or be different in some particular way according to the situation | *(c).* to make changes to sth to make it different to some extent

03 -- **vast** [adj.] -- extremely or unusually large, big or great in the area, amount, size, degree, etc. [*synonym*: immense]

04 -- **veal** [n.] -- meat from a young cow

05 -- **veer** [v.] -- *(a).* (especially of a vehicle) to change direction, course, position, inclination suddenly [*synonym*: swerve] | *(b).* (of a conversation, way of behaving/thinking) to suddenly change, opinion, subject, etc. from its normal course | *(c).* (of the wind) to change direction or its course

06 -- **vent** [v.] -- to express feelings of anger strongly || [n.] -- an opening allowing air, gas or liquid to pass

07 -- **vice** [n.] -- *(a).* criminal activities that involve prostitution or drugs | *(b).* immoral or wicked behavior or habits; an evil or immoral fault in sb's character

08 -- **vile** [adj.] -- *(a).* extremely unpleasant or bad [*synonym*: disgusting] | *(b).* extremely immoral and completely unacceptable [*synonym*: wicked]

09 -- void [v.] -- *(a).* (law) to state officially that sth is no longer valid or legal [*synonyms*: annul, invalidate, nullify] | *(b).* to empty waste substance from the bladder or bowels || **[adj.] --** *(a).* completely lacking or deficient in sth | *(b).* empty or unfilled | *(c).* (of a contract, an agreement, etc.) no longer valid or legal [*synonyms*: annulled, negated] || **[n.] --** a large empty space

4-Letter Words -- W

01 -- **wack** [adj.] -- *(a).* of very bad quality | *(b).* very strange

02 -- **wade** [v.] -- to walk with an effort through water or mud

03 -- **waft** [n.] -- a smell or a line of smoke moved or passed gently through the air | [v.] -- to move, or make sth such as sound, scent, smoke, etc. move, gently through the air [*synonym*: drift]

04 -- **wage** [v.] -- to begin and continue a battle, fight, war, etc. || [n.] -- the regular amount of money that a worker or service provider earns, hourly, daily, weekly or monthly

05 -- **waif** [n.] -- *(a).* very thin and weak child | *(b).* a homeless and neglected child [*synonym*: stray]

06 -- **wail** [v.] -- *(a).* to make a long, loud and high cry expressing sadness, suffering or pain [*synonym*: moan] | *(b).* to cry or complain about sth in a long, loud and high voice [*synonym*: moan] | *(c).* (of things) to make a sound that seems long, loud and high || [n.] -- a long, loud and high cry expressing sadness, suffering or pain [*synonym*: moan]

07 -- **wane** [v.] -- *(a).* to become gradually weaker, less important or less influential [*synonyms*: decrease, fade] | *(b).* (of the moon) to appear to be decreasing slightly in size each day after being round and full

08 -- **warp** [v.] -- *(a).* (of a surface or hard material) to become, or make sth become, twisted or bent out of its natural flat or straight shape, through too much heat or dampness [*synonyms*: distort, deform] | *(b).* to influence sb so that they start to behave in a shocking manner or in a manner that is unacceptable [*synonym*: pervert]

09 -- wart [n.] -- a small, hard, rough, dry raised area (lump) that grows on sb's skin on the face or other part of the body

10 -- wary [adj.] -- showing care, caution or mistrust when dealing with sb because there is the possibility of dangers or problems [*synonyms*: cautious, chary]

11 -- wavy [adj.] -- having curves [*synonyms*: curly, crumpled]

12 -- waxy [adj.] -- made of or covered with wax; looking or feeling like a wax

13 -- wean [v.] -- to cause a baby or young animal to stop feeding on its mother's milk or bottled milk and to start eating solid food

14 -- welt [n.] -- a raised mark on the skin due to hitting or rubbing [*synonym*: weal]

15 -- whee [excl.] -- used to express excitement

16 -- whet [v.] -- *(a).* to increase sb's desire for or interest in sth by giving them a small experience of it | *(b).* (of the edge of a knife or other tool) to sharpen by grinding or rubbing on or with sth such as a stone

17 -- whim [n.] -- a sudden unusual or unnecessary wish to do or have sth

18 -- whit [n.] -- a very small amount or of sth [synonyms: iota, speck]

19 -- wilt [v.] -- *(a).* (of a plant, leaf or flower) to bend towards the ground due to the disease, heat or a lack of water [*synonym*: droop] | *(b).* to lose strength and become tired or less confident [*synonym*: flag]

20 -- wily [adj.] -- clever at achieving or getting what you want, often through tricks [*synonym*: cunning]

21 -- wink [v.] -- *(a).* to close and open one eye very quickly, usually as an affection, hint, signal, joke, etc. | *(b).* to shine brightly with an unsteady light; to flash on and off [*synonym*: blink] || **[n.] --** an act of closing and opening one eye very quickly, usually as an affection, hint, signal, joke, etc.

22 -- wipe [v.] -- *(a).* to rub a surface lightly with a cloth, paper, your hand, etc. to remove dirt, food or liquid from it [*synonym*: mop] | *(b).* to remove dirt, food or liquid, etc. from a surface by rubbing it lightly with a cloth, paper, your hand, etc. | *(c).* to remove files from a computer or other digital device [*synonym*: erase] | *(d).* to deliberately forget an unpleasant or embarrassing experience [*synonym*: erase] || **[n.] --** *(a).* the action of rubbing a surface lightly with a cloth, paper, your hand, etc. to remove dirt, food or liquid from it | *(b).* the action of removing dirt, food or liquid, etc. from a surface by rubbing it lightly with a cloth, paper, your hand, etc. | *(c).* the action of removing files from a computer or other digital device

23 -- wiry [adj.] -- *(a).* (of a person) lean but strong [*synonym*: sinewy] | *(b).* (of hair, plants, etc.) thin, stiff and strong

24 -- wisp [n.] -- *(a).* a thin piece or small bundle of hair, grass, straw, hay, etc. | *(b).* a long thin line of smoke, mist or cloud

25 -- wonk [n.] -- *(a).* hardworking and boring person | *(b).* a person who is fond of political policy

26 -- writ [n.] -- a formal and legal order to do or not to do sth passed or issued by a court of law

4-Letter Words -- X, Y, Z

01 -- yank [v.] -- to pull sth/sb hard in a sudden and quick way [*synonym:* tug] || **[n.]** -- an act of pulling sth/sb hard in a sudden and quick way

02 -- yell [v.] -- to shout loudly because of anger, excitement, fear or pain [*synonyms*: scream, shriek] || **[n.]** -- *(a).* a loud cry of anger, excitement, fear or pain [*synonyms*: scream, shriek] | *(b).* an organized shout of support for a particular team

03 -- yelp [v.] -- to give a sudden, short, sharp, shrill cry of pain or alarm [*synonym*: yap] || **[n.]** -- a sudden, short, sharp, shrill cry of pain or alarm

04 -- yowl [v.] -- to make a long loud cry of unhappiness or pain [*synonym*: wail] || **[n.]** -- a long loud cry of unhappiness or pain [*synonym*: wail]

05 -- zany [adj.] -- strange, different or unusual in an amusing way [*synonym*: wacky]

06 -- zeal [n.] -- great energy, dedication, enthusiasm or eagerness for sth that you feel strongly about [*synonym*: fervor]

07 -- zing [v.] -- (a). to move or to make sth move very fast, with a high whistling sound | (b). to criticize sb strongly || **[n.]** -- energy, excitement, interest or liveliness

08 -- zoom [v.] -- *(a).* to move, go or travel somewhere very quickly [*synonyms*: rush, whizz] | *(b).* (of prices, costs, etc.) to increase a lot in a sudden and quick manner | *(c).* to make a loud, low-pitched, buzzing sound | *(d).* (of a camera or user) to change from a long shot to a close-up or the other way round || **[n.]** -- the sound of a vehicle moving very quickly

****

About the Author

Manik Joshi was born on January 26, 1979, at Ranikhet, a picturesque town in the Kumaon region of the Indian state of Uttarakhand. He is a permanent resident of the Sheeshmahal area of Kathgodam located in the city of Haldwani in the Kumaon region of Uttarakhand in India. He completed his schooling in four different schools. He is a science graduate in the ZBC – zoology, botany, and chemistry – subjects. He is also an MBA with a specialization in marketing. Additionally, he holds diplomas in "computer applications", "multimedia and web-designing", and "computer hardware and networking". During his schooldays, he wanted to enter the field of medical science; however, after graduation, he shifted his focus to the field of management. After obtaining his MBA, he enrolled in a computer education center; he became so fascinated with working on the computer that he decided to develop his career in this field. Over the following years, he worked at some computer-related full-time jobs. Following that, he became interested in Internet Marketing, particularly in domaining (business of buying and selling domain names), web design (creating websites), and various other online jobs. However, later he shifted his focus solely to self-publishing. Manik is a nature-lover. He has always been fascinated by overcast skies. He is passionate about traveling and enjoys solo travel most of the time rather than traveling in groups. He is actually quite a loner who prefers to do his own thing. He likes to listen to music, particularly when he is working on the computer. Reading and writing are definitely his favorite pastimes, but he has no interest in sports. Manik has always dreamed of a prosperous life and prefers to live a life of luxury. He has a keen interest in politics because he believes it is politics that decides everything else. He feels a sense of gratification sharing his experiences and knowledge with the outside world. However, he is an introvert by nature and thus gives prominence to only a few people in his personal life. He is not a spiritual man, yet he actively seeks knowledge about the metaphysical world; he is particularly interested in learning about life beyond death. In addition to writing academic/informational text and fictional content, he also maintains a personal diary. He has always had a desire to stand out from the crowd. He does not believe in treading the beaten path and avoids copying someone else's path to success. Two things he always refrains from are smoking and drinking; he is a teetotaler and very health-conscious. He usually wakes up before the sun rises. He starts his morning with meditation and exercise. Fitness is an integral and indispensable part of his life. He gets energized by solving complex problems. He loves himself the way he is and he loves the way he looks. He doesn't believe in following fashion trends. He dresses according to what suits him & what he is comfortable in. He believes in taking calculated risks. His philosophy is to expect the best but prepare for the worst. According to him, you can't succeed if you are unwilling to fail. For Manik, life is about learning from mistakes and figuring out how to move forward.

Amazon Author Page of Manik Joshi:
https://www.amazon.com/author/manikjoshi
Email: manik85joshi@gmail.com

BIBLIOGRAPHY

(A). SERIES TITLE: "ENGLISH DAILY USE" *[40 BOOKS]*

01. How to Start a Sentence
02. English Interrogative Sentences
03. English Imperative Sentences
04. Negative Forms In English
05. Learn English Exclamations
06. English Causative Sentences
07. English Conditional Sentences
08. Creating Long Sentences In English
09. How to Use Numbers In Conversation
10. Making Comparisons In English
11. Examples of English Correlatives
12. Interchange of Active and Passive Voice
13. Repetition of Words
14. Remarks In the English Language
15. Using Tenses In English
16. English Grammar- Am, Is, Are, Was, Were
17. English Grammar- Do, Does, Did
18. English Grammar- Have, Has, Had
19. English Grammar- Be and Have
20. English Modal Auxiliary Verbs
21. Direct and Indirect Speech
22. Get- Popular English Verb
23. Ending Sentences with Prepositions
24. Popular Sentences In English
25. Common English Sentences
26. Daily Use English Sentences
27. Speak English Sentences Every Day
28. Popular English Idioms and Phrases
29. Common English Phrases
30. Daily English- Important Notes
31. Collocations In the English Language
32. Words That Act as Multiple Parts of Speech (Part 1)
33. Words That Act as Multiple Parts of Speech (Part 2)
34. Nouns In the English Language
35. Regular and Irregular Verbs
36. Transitive and Intransitive Verbs

37. 10,000 Useful Adjectives In English
38. 4,000 Useful Adverbs In English
39. 20 Categories of Transitional Expressions
40. How to End a Sentence

****

(B). <u>SERIES</u> <u>TITLE</u>: "<u>ENGLISH</u> <u>WORD</u> <u>POWER</u>" *[30 <u>BOOKS</u>]*

01. Dictionary of English Synonyms
02. Dictionary of English Antonyms
03. Homonyms, Homophones and Homographs
04. Dictionary of English Capitonyms
05. Dictionary of Prefixes and Suffixes
06. Dictionary of Combining Forms
07. Dictionary of Literary Words
08. Dictionary of Old-fashioned Words
09. Dictionary of Humorous Words
10. Compound Words In English
11. Dictionary of Informal Words
12. Dictionary of Category Words
13. Dictionary of One-word Substitution
14. Hypernyms and Hyponyms
15. Holonyms and Meronyms
16. Oronym Words In English
17. Dictionary of Root Words
18. Dictionary of English Idioms
19. Dictionary of Phrasal Verbs
20. Dictionary of Difficult Words
21. Dictionary of Verbs
22. Dictionary of Adjectives
23. Dictionary of Adverbs
24. Dictionary of Formal Words
25. Dictionary of Technical Words
26. Dictionary of Foreign Words
27. Dictionary of Approving & Disapproving Words
28. Dictionary of Slang Words
29. Advanced English Phrases
30. Words In the English Language

****

(C). SERIES TITLE: "WORDS IN COMMON USAGE" [10 BOOKS]

01. How to Use the Word "Break" In English
02. How to Use the Word "Come" In English
03. How to Use the Word "Go" In English
04. How to Use the Word "Have" In English
05. How to Use the Word "Make" In English
06. How to Use the Word "Put" In English
07. How to Use the Word "Run" In English
08. How to Use the Word "Set" In English
09. How to Use the Word "Take" In English
10. How to Use the Word "Turn" In English

****

(D). SERIES TITLE: "WORDS BY NUMBER OF LETTERS" [10 BOOKS]

01. Dictionary of 4-Letter Words
02. Dictionary of 5-Letter Words
03. Dictionary of 6-Letter Words
04. Dictionary of 7-Letter Words
05. Dictionary of 8-Letter Words
06. Dictionary of 9-Letter Words
07. Dictionary of 10-Letter Words
08. Dictionary of 11-Letter Words
09. Dictionary of 12- to 14-Letter Words
10. Dictionary of 15- to 18-Letter Words

****

(E). SERIES TITLE: "ENGLISH WORKSHEETS" [10 BOOKS]

01. English Word Exercises (Part 1)
02. English Word Exercises (Part 2)
03. English Word Exercises (Part 3)
04. English Sentence Exercises (Part 1)
05. English Sentence Exercises (Part 2)
06. English Sentence Exercises (Part 3)
07. Test Your English
08. Match the Two Parts of the Words
09. Letter-Order In Words
10. Choose the Correct Spelling

Printed in Great Britain
by Amazon